W9-DGL-835

Reforming Planned
Economies in an
Integrating
World Economy

Integrating National Economies: Promise and Pitfalls

Barry Bosworth (Brookings Institution) and Gur Ofer (Hebrew University)
Reforming Planned Economies in an Integrating World Economy

Ralph C. Bryant (Brookings Institution)
International Coordination of National Stabilization Policies

Susan M. Collins (Brookings Institution/Georgetown University)
Distributive Issues: A Constraint on Global Integration

Richard N. Cooper (Harvard University)
Environment and Resource Policies for the World Economy

Ronald G. Ehrenberg (Cornell University)
Labor Markets and Integrating National Economies

Barry Eichengreen (University of California, Berkeley)
International Monetary Arrangements for the 21st Century

Mitsuhiro Fukao (Bank of Japan)
Financial Integration, Corporate Governance, and the Performance of Multinational Companies

Stephan Haggard (University of California, San Diego)
Developing Nations and the Politics of Global Integration

Richard J. Herring (University of Pennsylvania) and Robert E. Litan (Office of Management and Budget/Brookings Institution)
Financial Regulation in the Global Economy

Miles Kahler (University of California, San Diego)
International Institutions and the Political Economy of Integration

Anne O. Krueger (Stanford University)
Trade Policies and Developing Nations

Robert Z. Lawrence (Harvard University)
Regionalism, Multilateralism, and Deeper Integration

Sylvia Ostry (University of Toronto) and Richard R. Nelson (Columbia University)
Techno-Nationalism and Techno-Globalism: Conflict and Cooperation

Robert L. Paarlberg (Wellesley College/Harvard University)
Leadership Abroad Begins at Home: U.S. Foreign Economic Policy after the Cold War

Peter Rutland (Wesleyan University)
Russia, Eurasia, and the Global Economy

F. M. Scherer (Harvard University)
Competition Policies for an Integrated World Economy

Susan L. Shirk (University of California, San Diego)
How China Opened Its Door: The Political Success of the PRC's Foreign Trade and Investment Reforms

Alan O. Sykes (University of Chicago)
Product Standards for Internationally Integrated Goods Markets

Akihiko Tanaka (Institute of Oriental Culture, University of Tokyo)
The Politics of Deeper Integration: National Attitudes and Policies in Japan

Vito Tanzi (International Monetary Fund)
Taxation in an Integrating World

William Wallace (St. Antony's College, Oxford University)
Regional Integration: The West European Experience

Barry P. Bosworth and Gur Ofer

Reforming Planned Economies in an Integrating World Economy

THE BROOKINGS INSTITUTION
Washington, D.C.

Library of Congress Cataloging-in-Publication data:
Bosworth, Barry P., 1942–
Reforming planned economies in an integrating world economy /
Barry P. Bosworth and Gur Ofer
p. cm.—(Integrating national economies)
Includes bibliographical references and index.
ISBN 0-8157-1048-8 (alk. paper)—ISBN 0-8157-1047-X (pbk.)
1. Europe, Eastern—Economic policy—1989– 2. Europe, Central—
Economic policy. 3. Post-communism—Economic aspects—Europe,
Eastern. 4. Post-communism—Economic aspects—Europe, Central.
5. China—Economic policy—1976– I. Ofer, Gur. II. Title.
III. Series.
HC244.B699 1995
338.947—dc20 95-3848
CIP

9 8 7 6 5 4 3 2 1

The paper used in this publication meets the minimum requirements of
American National Standard for Information Sciences—Permanence of Paper
for Printed Library Materials, ANSI Z39.48-1984

Typeset in Plantin

Composition by Princeton Editorial Associates
Princeton, New Jersey

Printed by R. R. Donnelley and Sons Co.
Harrisonburg, Virginia

Foreword

THE formerly centrally planned economies are making historic changes as they attempt to convert to Western-style market economies based on private enterprise. This transition requires that they change their way of thinking about economic issues and almost completely rebuild their principal economic institutions. To date, the results of the reform process range from amazing success in China to economic and political disarray in the states of the former Soviet Union. In the latter, the optimism that swelled in the aftermath of the peaceful overthrow of communism has given way to a more sober assessment of the challenges these countries face.

A major part of the transition involves the efforts of the countries in central Europe and the former Soviet Union to join the mainstream of the global economy through expanded economic relations with other nations. Particularly in Europe, the transitional economies are seeking entry into a regional trading system at a time when many of the other countries are attempting to move beyond the traditional emphasis on trade in goods to a deeper economic integration involving trade in services, the free flow of financial capital, and the adoption of common institutions and rules governing their economies. At issue is whether the formerly centrally planned economies can successfully participate in such an expanded economic system, given the still rudimentary nature of their institutions.

Barry Bosworth and Gur Ofer review the progress that the formerly centrally planned economies have made in establishing markets and the institutions required to support them. They examine the changes in their foreign economic institutions and pattern of trade that have emerged in the first few years of the reform process. The authors highlight the chief issues that any successful reform program must address and emphasize the extent to which numerous changes in both domestic and foreign economic activities are interrelated and mutually reinforcing. In their assessment they draw sharp distinctions among China, Central Europe, and the states of the former Soviet Union. They argue that, although reform of the external trade regime is critical, the major barriers to a rapid and successful transition to a market-based economy and the growth of external trade are mostly domestic. Surprising progress has been made in just a few years, but it now appears that catching up to other countries will take decades.

Barry Bosworth is a senior fellow in Economic Studies at the Brookings Institution, and Gur Ofer is professor of economics at the Hebrew University in Jerusalem. Hillary Sheldon and Marc Steinberg provided invaluable research assistance. The authors are indebted to the participants in a Brookings review conference on January 13–14, 1994, and to their discussants, Alan Gelb and Richard Portes, for constructive criticism and helpful suggestions. Princeton Editorial Associates edited the manuscript and prepared the index. Laura Kelly verified its factual content. Sara Hufham assisted in editing the reference list.

Funding for this project was provided by the Center for Global Partnership of the Japan Foundation, the Curry Foundation, the Ford Foundation, the Korea Foundation, the Alfred P. Sloan Foundation, the Tokyo Foundation for Global Studies, the United States–Japan Foundation, and the Alex C. Walker Educational and Charitable Foundation.

The views expressed in this book are those of the authors and should not be ascribed to any of the persons or organizations acknowledged above, or to the trustees, officers, or staff members of the Brookings Institution.

BRUCE K. MACLAURY
President

March 1995
Washington, D.C.

Contents

Tables

Figures

Preface to the Studies on Integrating National Economies

E CONOMIC interdependence among nations has increased sharply in the past half century. For example, while the value of total production of industrial countries increased at a rate of about 9 percent a year on average between 1964 and 1992, the value of the exports of those nations grew at an average rate of 12 percent, and lending and borrowing across national borders through banks surged upward even more rapidly at 23 percent a year. This international economic interdependence has contributed to significantly improved standards of living for most countries. Continuing international economic integration holds out the promise of further benefits. Yet the increasing sensitivity of national economies to events and policies originating abroad creates dilemmas and pitfalls if national policies and international cooperation are poorly managed.

The Brookings Project on Integrating National Economies, of which this study is a component, focuses on the interplay between two fundamental facts about the world at the end of the twentieth century. First, the world will continue for the foreseeable future to be organized politically into nation-states with sovereign governments. Second, increasing economic integration among nations will continue to erode differences among national economies and undermine the autonomy of national governments. The project explores the opportunities and tensions arising from these two facts.

Scholars from a variety of disciplines have produced twenty-one studies for the first phase of the project. Each study examines the heightened competition between national political sovereignty and increased cross-border economic integration. This preface identifies background themes and issues common to all the studies and provides a brief overview of the project as a whole.[1]

Increasing World Economic Integration

Two underlying sets of causes have led nations to become more closely intertwined. First, technological, social, and cultural changes have sharply reduced the effective economic distances among nations. Second, many of the government policies that traditionally inhibited cross-border transactions have been relaxed or even dismantled.

The same improvements in transportation and communications technology that make it much easier and cheaper for companies in New York to ship goods to California, for residents of Strasbourg to visit relatives in Marseilles, and for investors in Hokkaido to buy and sell shares on the Tokyo Stock Exchange facilitate trade, migration, and capital movements spanning nations and continents. The sharply reduced costs of moving goods, money, people, and information underlie the profound economic truth that technology has made the world markedly smaller.

New communications technology has been especially significant for financial activity. Computers, switching devices, and telecommunications satellites have slashed the cost of transmitting information internationally, of confirming transactions, and of paying for transactions. In the 1950s, for example, foreign exchange could be bought and sold only during conventional business hours in the initiating party's time zone. Such transactions can now be carried out instantaneously twenty-four hours a day. Large banks pass the management of their worldwide foreign-exchange positions around the globe from one branch to another, staying continuously ahead of the setting sun.

Such technological innovations have increased the knowledge of potentially profitable international exchanges and of economic opportunities abroad. Those developments, in turn, have changed consumers' and producers' tastes. Foreign goods, foreign vacations, foreign financial investments—virtually anything from other nations—have lost some of their exotic character.

---

1. A complete list of authors and study titles is included at the beginning of this volume, facing the title page.

Although technological change permits increased contact among nations, it would not have produced such dramatic effects if it had been countermanded by government policies. Governments have traditionally taxed goods moving in international trade, directly restricted imports and subsidized exports, and tried to limit international capital movements. Those policies erected "separation fences" at the borders of nations. From the perspective of private sector agents, separation fences imposed extra costs on cross-border transactions. They reduced trade and, in some cases, eliminated it. During the 1930s governments used such policies with particular zeal, a practice now believed to have deepened and lengthened the Great Depression.

After World War II, most national governments began—sometimes unilaterally, more often collaboratively—to lower their separation fences, to make them more permeable, or sometimes even to tear down parts of them. The multilateral negotiations under the auspices of the General Agreement on Trade and Tariffs (GATT)—for example, the Kennedy Round in the 1960s, the Tokyo Round in the 1970s, and most recently the protracted negotiations of the Uruguay Round, formally signed only in April 1994—stand out as the most prominent examples of fence lowering for trade in goods. Though contentious and marked by many compromises, the GATT negotiations are responsible for sharp reductions in at-the-border restrictions on trade in goods and services. After the mid-1980s a large number of developing countries moved unilaterally to reduce border barriers and to pursue outwardly oriented policies.

The lowering of fences for financial transactions began later and was less dramatic. Nonetheless, by the 1990s government restrictions on capital flows, especially among the industrial countries, were much less important and widespread than at the end of World War II and in the 1950s.

By shrinking the economic distances among nations, changes in technology would have progressively integrated the world economy even in the absence of reductions in governments' separation fences. Reductions in separation fences would have enhanced interdependence even without the technological innovations. Together, these two sets of evolutionary changes have reinforced each other and strikingly transformed the world economy.

Changes in the Government of Nations

Simultaneously with the transformation of the global economy, major changes have occurred in the world's political structure. First, the number of governmental decisionmaking units in the world has expanded markedly and political power has been diffused more broadly among them. Rising nationalism and, in some areas, heightened ethnic tensions have accompanied that increasing political pluralism.

The history of membership in international organizations documents the sharp growth in the number of independent states. For example, only 44 nations participated in the Bretton Woods conference of July 1944, which gave birth to the International Monetary Fund. But by the end of 1970, the IMF had 118 member nations. The number of members grew to 150 by the mid-1980s and to 178 by December 1993. Much of this growth reflects the collapse of colonial empires. Although many nations today are small and carry little individual weight in the global economy, their combined influence is considerable and their interests cannot be ignored as easily as they were in the past.

A second political trend, less visible but equally important, has been the gradual loss of the political and economic hegemony of the United States. Immediately after World War II, the United States by itself accounted for more than one-third of world production. By the early 1990s the U.S. share had fallen to about one-fifth. Concurrently, the political and economic influence of the European colonial powers continued to wane, and the economic significance of nations outside Europe and North America, such as Japan, Korea, Indonesia, China, Brazil, and Mexico, increased. A world in which economic power and influence are widely diffused has displaced a world in which one or a few nations effectively dominated international decisionmaking.

Turmoil and the prospect of fundamental change in the formerly centrally planned economies compose a third factor causing radical changes in world politics. During the era of central planning, governments in those nations tried to limit external influences on their economies. Now leaders in the formerly planned economies are trying to adopt reforms modeled on Western capitalist principles. To the extent that these efforts succeed, those nations will increase their economic involvement with the rest of the world. Political and economic alignments among the Western industrialized nations will be forced to adapt.

Governments and scholars have begun to assess these three trends, but their far-reaching ramifications will not be clear for decades.

Dilemmas for National Policies

Cross-border economic integration and national political sovereignty have increasingly come into conflict, leading to a growing mismatch between the economic and political structures of the world. The effective domains of economic markets have come to coincide less and less with national governmental jurisdictions.

When the separation fences at nations' borders were high, governments and citizens could sharply distinguish "international" from "domestic" policies. International policies dealt with at-the-border barriers, such as tariffs and quotas, or responded to events occurring abroad. In contrast, domestic policies were concerned with everything behind the nation's borders, such as competition and antitrust rules, corporate governance, product standards, worker safety, regulation and supervision of financial institutions, environmental protection, tax codes, and the government's budget. Domestic policies were regarded as matters about which nations were sovereign, to be determined by the preferences of the nation's citizens and its political institutions, without regard for effects on other nations.

As separation fences have been lowered and technological innovations have shrunk economic distances, a multitude of formerly neglected differences among nations' domestic policies have become exposed to international scrutiny. National governments and international negotiations must thus increasingly deal with "deeper"—behind-the-border—integration. For example, if country A permits companies to emit air and water pollutants whereas country B does not, companies that use pollution-generating methods of production will find it cheaper to produce in country A. Companies in country B that compete internationally with companies in country A are likely to complain that foreign competitors enjoy unfair advantages and to press for international pollution standards.

Deeper integration requires analysis of the economic and the political aspects of virtually all nonborder policies and practices. Such

issues have already figured prominently in negotiations over the evolution of the European Community, over the Uruguay Round of
GATT negotiations, over the North American Free Trade Agreement
(NAFTA), and over the bilateral economic relationships between
Japan and the United States. Future debates about behind-the-border
policies will occur with increasing frequency and prove at least as
complex and contentious as the past negotiations regarding at-the-
border restrictions.

Tensions about deeper integration arise from three broad sources:
cross-border spillovers, diminished national autonomy, and challenges
to political sovereignty.

Cross-Border Spillovers

Some activities in one nation produce consequences that spill
across borders and affect other nations. Illustrations of these spillovers abound. Given the impact of modern technology of banking
and securities markets in creating interconnected networks, lax rules
in one nation erode the ability of all other nations to enforce banking
and securities rules and to deal with fraudulent transactions. Given
the rapid diffusion of knowledge, science and technology policies in
one nation generate knowledge that other nations can use without full
payment. Labor market policies become matters of concern to other
nations because workers migrate in search of work; policies in one
nation can trigger migration that floods or starves labor markets
elsewhere. When one nation dumps pollutants into the air or water
that other nations breathe or drink, the matter goes beyond the
unitary concern of the polluting nation and becomes a matter for
international negotiation. Indeed, the hydrocarbons that are emitted
into the atmosphere when individual nations burn coal for generating
electricity contribute to global warming and are thereby a matter of
concern for the entire world.

The tensions associated with cross-border spillovers can be especially vexing when national policies generate outcomes alleged to be
competitively inequitable, as in the example in which country A
permits companies to emit pollutants and country B does not. Or
consider a situation in which country C requires commodities, whether
produced at home or abroad, to meet certain design standards, justified for safety reasons. Foreign competitors may find it too expensive

to meet these standards. In that event, the standards in C act very much like tariffs or quotas, effectively narrowing or even eliminating foreign competition for domestic producers. Citing examples of this sort, producers or governments in individual nations often complain that business is not conducted on a "level playing field." Typically, the complaining nation proposes that *other* nations adjust their policies to moderate or remove the competitive inequities.

Arguments for creating a level playing field are troublesome at best. International trade occurs precisely because of differences among nations—in resource endowments, labor skills, and consumer tastes. Nations specialize in producing goods and services in which they are relatively most efficient. In a fundamental sense, cross-border trade is valuable because the playing field is *not* level.

When David Ricardo first developed the theory of comparative advantage, he focused on differences among nations owing to climate or technology. But Ricardo could as easily have ascribed the productive differences to differing "social climates" as to physical or technological climates. Taking all "climatic" differences as given, the theory of comparative advantage argues that free trade among nations will maximize global welfare.

Taken to its logical extreme, the notion of leveling the playing field implies that nations should become homogeneous in all major respects. But that recommendation is unrealistic and even pernicious. Suppose country A decides that it is too poor to afford the costs of a clean environment, and will thus permit the production of goods that pollute local air and water supplies. Or suppose it concludes that it cannot afford stringent protections for worker safety. Country A will then argue that it is inappropriate for other nations to impute to country A the value they themselves place on a clean environment and safety standards (just as it would be inappropriate to impute the A valuations to the environment of other nations). The core of the idea of political sovereignty is to permit national residents to order their lives and property in accord with their own preferences.

Which perspective about differences among nations in behind-the-border policies is more compelling? Is country A merely exercising its national preferences and appropriately exploiting its comparative advantage in goods that are dirty or dangerous to produce? Or does a legitimate international problem exist that justifies pressure from other nations urging country A to accept changes in its policies (thus curbing its national sovereignty)? When national governments negotiate resolutions to such questions—trying to agree whether individual nations are legitimately exercising sovereign choices or, alternatively, engaging in behavior that is unfair or damaging to other nations—the dialogue is invariably contentious because the resolutions depend on the typically complex circumstances of the international spillovers and on the relative weights accorded to the interests of particular individuals and particular nations.

Diminished National Autonomy

As cross-border economic integration increases, governments experience greater difficulties in trying to control events within their borders. Those difficulties, summarized by the term *diminished autonomy*, are the second set of reasons why tensions arise from the competition between political sovereignty and economic integration.

For example, nations adjust monetary and fiscal policies to influence domestic inflation and employment. In setting these policies, smaller countries have always been somewhat constrained by foreign economic events and policies. Today, however, all nations are constrained, often severely. More than in the past, therefore, nations may be better able to achieve their economic goals if they work together collaboratively in adjusting their macroeconomic policies.

Diminished autonomy and cross-border spillovers can sometimes be allowed to persist without explicit international cooperation to deal with them. States in the United States adopt their own tax systems and set policies for assistance to poor single people without any formal cooperation or limitation. Market pressures operate to force a degree of de facto cooperation. If one state taxes corporations too heavily, it knows business will move elsewhere. (Those familiar with older debates about "fiscal federalism" within the United States and other nations will recognize the similarity between those issues and the emerging international debates about deeper integration of national economies.) Analogously, differences among nations in regulations, standards, policies, institutions, and even social and cultural preferences create economic incentives for a kind of arbitrage that erodes or eliminates the differences. Such pressures involve not only the conventional arbitrage that exploits price differentials (buying at one point in geographic space or time and selling at another) but also shifts in the location of production facilities and in the residence of factors of production.

In many other cases, however, cross-border spillovers, arbitrage pressures, and diminished effectiveness of national policies can produce unwanted consequences. In cases involving what economists call externalities (external economies and diseconomies), national governments may need to cooperate to promote mutual interests. For example, population growth, continued urbanization, and the more intensive exploitation of natural resources generate external diseconomies not only within but across national boundaries. External economies generated when benefits spill across national jurisdictions probably also increase in importance (for instance, the gains from basic research and from control of communicable diseases).

None of these situations is new, but technological change and the reduction of tariffs and quotas heighten their importance. When one nation produces goods (such as scientific research) or "bads" (such as pollution) that significantly affect other nations, individual governments acting sequentially and noncooperatively cannot deal effectively with the resulting issues. In the absence of explicit cooperation and political leadership, too few collective goods and too many collective bads will be supplied.

Challenges to Political Sovereignty

The pressures from cross-border economic integration sometimes even lead individuals or governments to challenge the core assumptions of national political sovereignty. Such challenges are a third source of tensions about deeper integration.

The existing world system of nation-states assumes that a nation's residents are free to follow their own values and to select their own political arrangements without interference from others. Similarly, property rights are allocated by nation. (The so-called global commons, such as outer space and the deep seabed, are the sole exceptions.) A nation is assumed to have the sovereign right to exploit its property in accordance with its own preferences and policies. Political sovereignty is thus analogous to the concept of consumer sovereignty (the presumption that the individual consumer best knows his or her own interests and should exercise them freely).

In times of war, some nations have had sovereignty wrested from them by force. In earlier eras, a handful of individuals or groups have questioned the premises of political sovereignty. With the profound increases in economic integration in recent decades, however, a larger number of individuals and groups—and occasionally even their national governments—have identified circumstances in which, it is claimed, some universal or international set of values should take precedence over the preferences or policies of particular nations.

Some groups seize on human-rights issues, for example, or what they deem to be egregiously inappropriate political arrangements in other nations. An especially prominent case occurred when citizens in many nations labeled the former apartheid policies of South Africa an affront to universal values and emphasized that the South African government was not legitimately representing the interests of a majority of South Africa's residents. Such views caused many national governments to apply economic sanctions against South Africa. Examples of value conflicts are not restricted to human rights, however. Groups focusing on environmental issues characterize tropical rain forests as the lungs of the world and the genetic repository for numerous species of plants and animals that are the heritage of all mankind. Such views lead Europeans, North Americans, or Japanese to challenge the timber-cutting policies of Brazilians and Indonesians. A recent controversy over tuna fishing with long drift nets that kill porpoises is yet another example. Environmentalists in the United States whose sensibilities were offended by the drowning of porpoises required U.S. boats at some additional expense to amend their fishing practices. The U.S. fishermen, complaining about imported tuna caught with less regard for porpoises, persuaded the U.S. government to ban such tuna imports (both direct imports from the countries in which the tuna is caught and indirect imports shipped via third countries). Mexico and Venezuela were the main countries affected by this ban; a GATT dispute panel sided with Mexico against the United States in the controversy, which further upset the U.S. environmental community.

A common feature of all such examples is the existence, real or alleged, of "psychological externalities" or "political failures." Those holding such views reject untrammeled political sovereignty for nation-states in deference to universal or non-national values. They wish to constrain the exercise of individual nations' sovereignties through international negotiations or, if necessary, by even stronger intervention.

The Management of International Convergence

In areas in which arbitrage pressures and cross-border spillovers are weak and psychological or political externalities are largely absent, national governments may encounter few problems with deeper integration. Diversity across nations may persist quite easily. But at the other extreme, arbitrage and spillovers in some areas may be so strong that they threaten to erode national diversity completely. Or psychological and political sensitivities may be asserted too powerfully to be ignored. Governments will then be confronted with serious tensions, and national policies and behaviors may eventually converge to common, worldwide patterns (for example, subject to internationally agreed norms or minimum standards). Eventual convergence across nations, if it occurs, could happen in a harmful way (national policies and practices being driven to a least common denominator with externalities ignored, in effect a "race to the bottom") or it could occur with mutually beneficial results ("survival of the fittest and the best").

Each study in this series addresses basic questions about the management of international convergence: if, when, and how national governments should intervene to try to influence the consequences of arbitrage pressures, cross-border spillovers, diminished autonomy, and the assertion of psychological or political externalities. A wide variety of responses is conceivable. We identify six, which should be regarded not as distinct categories but as ranges along a continuum.

National autonomy defines a situation at one end of the continuum in which national governments make decentralized decisions with little or no consultation and no explicit cooperation. This response represents political sovereignty at its strongest, undiluted by any international management of convergence.

Mutual recognition, like national autonomy, presumes decentralized decisions by national governments and relies on market competition to guide the process of international convergence. Mutual recognition, however, entails exchanges of information and consultations among governments to constrain the formation of national regulations and policies. As understood in discussions of economic integration within the European Community, moreover, mutual recognition entails an explicit acceptance by each member nation of the regulations, standards, and certification procedures of other members. For example, mutual recognition allows wine or liquor produced in any European Union country to be sold in all twelve member countries even if production standards in member countries differ. Doctors licensed in France are permitted to practice in Germany, and vice versa, even if licensing procedures in the two countries differ.

Governments may agree on rules that restrict their freedom to set policy or that promote gradual convergence in the structure of policy. As international consultations and monitoring of compliance with such rules become more important, this situation can be described as *monitored decentralization*. The Group of Seven finance ministers meetings, supplemented by the IMF's surveillance over exchange rate and macroeconomic policies, illustrate this approach to management.

Coordination goes further than mutual recognition and monitored decentralization in acknowledging convergence pressures. It is also more ambitious in promoting intergovernmental cooperation to deal with them. Coordination involves jointly designed mutual adjustments of national policies. In clear-cut cases of coordination, bargaining occurs and governments agree to behave differently from the ways they would have behaved without the agreement. Examples include the World Health Organization's procedures for controlling communicable diseases and the 1987 Montreal Protocol (to a 1985 framework convention) for the protection of stratospheric ozone by reducing emissions of chlorofluorocarbons.

Explicit harmonization, which requires still higher levels of intergovernmental cooperation, may require agreement on regional standards or world standards. Explicit harmonization typically entails still greater departures from decentralization in decisionmaking and still further strengthening of international institutions. The 1988 agreement among major central banks to set minimum standards for the required capital positions of commercial banks (reached through the Committee on Banking Regulations and Supervisory Practices at the Bank for International Settlements) is an example of partially harmonized regulations.

At the opposite end of the spectrum from national autonomy lies *federalist mutual governance*, which implies continuous bargaining and joint, centralized decisionmaking. To make federalist mutual governance work would require greatly strengthened supranational institutions. This end of the management spectrum, now relevant only as an analytical benchmark, is a possible outcome that can be imagined for the middle or late decades of the twenty-first century, possibly even sooner for regional groupings like the European Union.

Overview of the Brookings Project

Despite their growing importance, the issues of deeper economic integration and its competition with national political sovereignty were largely neglected in the 1980s. In 1992 the Brookings Institution initiated its project on Integrating National Economies to direct attention to these important questions.

In studying this topic, Brookings sought and received the co-operation of some of the world's leading economists, political scientists, foreign-policy specialists, and government officials, representing all regions of the world. Although some functional areas require a special focus on European, Japanese, and North American perspectives, at all junctures the goal was to include, in addition, the perspectives of developing nations and the formerly centrally planned economies.

The first phase of the project commissioned the twenty-one scholarly studies listed at the beginning of the book. One or two lead discussants, typically residents of parts of the world other than the area where the author resides, were asked to comment on each study.

Authors enjoyed substantial freedom to design their individual studies, taking due account of the overall themes and goals of the project. The guidelines for the studies requested that at least some of the analysis be carried out with a non-normative perspective. In effect, authors were asked to develop a "baseline" of what might happen in the absence of changed policies or further international cooperation. For their normative analyses, authors were asked to start with an agnostic posture that did not prejudge the net benefits or costs resulting from integration. The project organizers themselves had no presumption about whether national diversity is better or worse than international convergence or about what the individual studies should conclude regarding the desirability of increased integration. On the contrary, each author was asked to address the trade-offs in his or her issue area between diversity and convergence and to locate the area, currently and prospectively, on

the spectrum of international management possibilities running between national autonomy through mutual recognition to coordination
and explicit harmonization.

HENRY J. AARON   SUSAN M. COLLINS
RALPH C. BRYANT   ROBERT Z. LAWRENCE

Chapter 1

Economic Integration in the Formerly Centrally Planned Economies

*T*HE CHALLENGE to transform the formerly centrally planned economies (CPEs) into market-based, private enterprise systems has
created both opportunities and problems of historic magnitude. After
more than forty years of extreme autarky (seventy years for some
republics of the former Soviet Union), these countries are trying to
join the mainstream of the global economy through a radical internal
restructuring and participation in international trade and financial
systems. The transformation is proving to be a far more daunting task
than supposed just a few years ago: the countries must create a host
of new institutions and specify the rules under which they should
operate while simultaneously preventing a collapse of economic output and living standards. Some of their initial optimism has disap-
peared, output has fallen sharply, inflation has worsened, and the process
of reform has become mired in political debate. For some countries,
what was once seen as a transition has been more like starting over.

Yet many countries have made substantial progress in establishing
the basic framework of a market economy. For Central Europe and
the Baltics, the worst of the adjustment appears to be past and
economic recovery is under way. The private sector is growing, and
the composition of production is shifting toward services and consumer products. While output is still declining in Russia, markets have
been liberalized, and privatization is occurring on a massive scale. China,
over a longer period of transition, has achieved remarkable economic
growth while gradually moving toward a market-based system.

As economic development moves forward in these countries, it will
have a considerable effect on the global economy, altering prior

1

patterns of trade and exerting significant pressure on international financial markets. In time, it will greatly change the path of economic integration within Europe. It has already raised the specter of greatly increased immigration.

History provides little guidance on how best to accomplish such a transition. Although Western economists can list the essential characteristics of a market economy and outline the principal changes that must take place, they are unable to explain precisely how to move from one system to another and the optimal sequence in which the reforms should be undertaken. Since few economists in the West are familiar with the operation of centrally planned economies, their initial suggestions for reform have taken little account of the missing institutions and the lags involved in creating them. Nor have they been able to make judgments about the political feasibility of specific policies. There is now a growing appreciation that the process of reform will involve more trial and error than originally believed; that it will be driven by internal political, social, and economic decisions; and that the contribution of outsiders will be limited.

The purpose of this volume is to examine the economic transition in relation to the global economy. Two questions of particular interest here are what role will external economic integration play in the internal transition, and what position are these countries likely to hold in the global economy? The discussion proceeds on the assumption that internal and external reforms are intimately tied together and therefore can be evaluated only in combination. Fundamentally, economic integration means expanding markets from the national to the global level; but the economies in transition lack even the basic institutions required to operate an internal market economy. Unless they can change the structure of the domestic economy and the incentive system, they will not be able to participate in the global economy to any extent, and the benefits they can derive from a larger market will be extremely limited.

Economic integration occurs at several levels. At the level traditionally known as "shallow integration," it takes the form of an expansion of trade in goods and services, capital flows, direct investment, and the transfer of technologies. The predominant concerns at this level are trade liberalization, current account convertibility, capital account convertibility, and the sequence in which those actions should be undertaken. Deeper levels of integration involve the creation of legal, regulatory, and social institutions that conform to global norms. Whatever the level being attempted, the transitional economies, with their tradition of economic autarky and tight controls over the flow of information, start from very far behind. The question is, can they catch up by skipping some of the evolutionary stages through which other countries have passed and by adopting at the outset the regulations and institutions required to achieve deep integration with the global economy? This issue is relevant not only for Central European countries that envision a future of deep regional integration with the European Union, but also for the states of the former Soviet Union, if they should choose to build on the base of the extensive trade they used to engage in as republics of that union.[1]

In their search for historical precedents, some analysts have compared the problems of these economies with those faced by Western Europe and Japan after World War II. But we are rapidly learning that transforming an economic system from one kind to another is quite different from rebuilding the capital stock of postwar Europe. Moreover, the external world economy has changed drastically since the 1950s. It is now far more sophisticated, with a greater volume of external trade in goods and services, established networks of producers and distributors, and a more complex international financial system. Thus another interesting point to consider is whether these advances will make it easier or harder for the countries in transition to restructure their economies and develop effective economic relations with other countries.[2] Will they be able gain access to markets for their exports and compete for scarce capital in international financial markets? Also in contrast with the situation in the 1950s, the countries of Central Europe and the former Soviet Union have been trying to expand their position in the global trading system at a time of weak growth and growing unemployment in the major markets of Western Europe.

1. The former Soviet Union is now represented by fifteen independent states. The three Baltic states have broken sharply with the others and are in many respects more similar to the Central European economies. The remaining twelve states are loosely linked through the Commonwealth of Independent States (CIS).

2. It is also tempting to compare the situation in these countries with that in several countries of Latin America. Certainly, these countries are similar in their vulnerability to inflation. And the former can learn much about the design of stabilization programs from the experience of the latter. They are much different, however, on the supply side in that the former lack the normal institutions of a market economy. Thus the reaction of the economic system to traditional stabilization policies is often much different than expected.

The countries of interest here can be usefully compared in terms of the progress they have made first in developing coherent strategies for converting to market-based economies, and second in actually implementing those programs. On that basis, the countries can be divided into three groups: the smaller economies of Central and Eastern Europe, which are attempting to integrate as quickly as possible with the global economy; China, which has chosen more gradual reform through a two-tracked strategy of developing a nonstate, semiprivate sector based on the creation of new enterprises while maintaining the large state enterprises within the old system of central control; and the republics of the former Soviet Union, which are still struggling to find a coherent approach to economic reform.[3]

The economies of Central Europe are all quite small and lacking in natural resources, except for an unusually well-educated work force. If they are to achieve the efficiencies and living standards of Western Europe, they need the economies of scale and specialization that can only be achieved by integrating into a large regional or global trading system. Their governments seem to agree with international institutions suggesting that they follow a development strategy not unlike that being recommended to developing economies in Latin America and Asia: namely, liberalize the domestic economy and open it to the global economy. On the external side, that means establishing the convertibility of their currencies for current account transactions, and soon thereafter for capital transactions. Internally, the emphasis is on building the institutions of a market system and on privatizing the existing state enterprises. Most of these countries have made some progress in implementing this strategy and are aiming for a particularly high degree of economic integration with Western Europe. The debate surrounding their actions is largely about the speed of reform, not the reform agenda.

In contrast, China has rejected much of the Western advice about internal economic liberalization. For example, it has made no extensive effort to privatize the large state enterprises. But it has placed

---

3. The countries of the former Soviet Union are economically diverse, although Russia is a special case. The Baltic states are more similar to Central Europe. A few—such as Turkmenistan, Kazakhstan, and Azerbaijan—are rich in natural resources. Many could prosper only in close cooperation with other republics.

great emphasis on developing a parallel semiprivate economy based on joint ventures with foreign firms and on establishing township and village enterprises free from state control. Its external liberalization has occurred mainly in the area of trade (current account convertibility) and has excluded financial transactions (capital account convertibility). China has been able to maintain a stable macroeconomic environment and strong political control while still creating an economic climate at the local level conducive to economic change and growth. Strictly from an economic perspective, the Chinese transformation over the past decade has been remarkably successful; but important questions have been raised about the contribution of specific reforms, such as trade liberalization and the management of the state enterprises during the transition period.

The greatest problems, but also the most interesting policy questions, arise in the republics of the former Soviet Union. Their economies have suffered larger declines in output and living standards than those of Central Europe; and even more discouraging, the situation is unlikely to change in the near future. Unlike Central Europe, Russia and some of the other former Soviet republics are extraordinarily rich in natural resources. They also constituted a large and quite integrated economy before the breakup of the USSR. However, they face far more severe political problems than the other transitional economies.

These countries differ from China in the extent of their industrialization and in their previously high level of intrarepublic trade. The Chinese provinces engaged in only low levels of trade and emphasized a high degree of local self-sufficiency. If the Soviet Union often pushed economies of plant size beyond reasonable limits, China was at the other extreme of suboptimal production.

With the economic and political disintegration of the USSR, it became impossible to adopt a transition strategy similar to that of China, but the republics could not follow Central Europe, either. Given the size of the Russian economy and the extensive trade between the republics in the 1980s, their internal restructuring and regional integration, both in trade and financial transactions, take on greater importance. Nevertheless, the external economy will still exert pressure for change and have an effect on prices, technology, services, and trade.

The Legacy of the Past

The nature of the economic transition taking place in these countries cannot be understood without some knowledge of its starting point. Initially, the legacy from the old system—which consisted of a well-educated work force and a level of economic performance between that of the industrial countries and the best-performing developing economies—was seen as a potential plus. One study in 1990, reflecting the early optimism, projected that GDP would grow in the neighborhood of 7 percent a year, aided by enormous inflows of foreign capital.[4] In the span of just a few years, that legacy came to be perceived more as a net negative, raising the possibility that growth in the transitional economies may fall short of that of other regions for many years. Not only are the transitional economies plagued with an outdated stock of capital, but they have inherited a set of institutions and attitudes particularly poorly suited for competing in a modern global economy. The influence of that legacy casts a large shadow on any projections about the future.[5]

Central Planning

The starting point for all the economies in question was centralized planning. Couched in commands and detailed coordinating instructions, it filtered down through each country's hierarchical structure of authority. That structure was composed of enterprises, associations, ministries, and the central planning office. As information flowed up and down this structure, it underwent numerous adjustments. The end result was a set of detailed central orders to each enterprise on all relevant aspects of its operations. The state ministries were organized around specific industries or branches of industries. Thus the organizational system contributed to the development of monopolies as each ministry was responsible for the entire output of an industry, even in a country as vast as the Soviet Union.

Under this system, all internal and external trade was mapped out and imposed on enterprises by the central plan. The enterprises did

4. Centre for Economic Policy Research (1990).
5. Beenstock (1992) provides some evidence that the scars of history never fade away and that the legacy of a half century of communism will exert a negative influence for a very long time.

not act as independent entities responsible for their own future. In most cases, quantities, prices, buyers, and suppliers were all predetermined. Only households could choose whether to buy what was available in stores, a choice restricted by the narrow range of options. The allocative and competitive function of prices played a limited role, being relevant perhaps only as far as the planners themselves were concerned. Even at the planning level, many prices were distorted, not only in relation to world prices, but also in relation to the real costs to the domestic economy.

In practice, the system never worked quite as described, and, particularly in the Soviet Union, an enormous network of bureaucrats in government ministries and the Communist party acted to coordinate its activities and relieve bottlenecks. Party officials served as expeditors, helping plant managers resolve delivery delays; as a result, the economic plan, which was supposed to govern production, underwent continuous modifications. But with decentralization and the decline in the power and influence of the party in the late 1980s, the system lost its coordinating mechanism.

The most obvious failure of the system was the poor quality of domestic products in comparison with those available in the global market, a consequence of the lack of competition in what amounted to the most extreme version of sellers' markets. The central planners were continually experimenting with alternative incentive schemes to improve quality, expand the product mix, and cut costs in an attempt to simulate the results achieved automatically through competition in market economies. They were nearly always circumvented by producers.

The emphasis on administrative control also led to the suppression of a large range of business services that are normally required to facilitate the operation of markets. These include accounting, financial services, specialists in international trade, and lawyers. For example, these economies had no true financial system. The banks were simply a passive extension of the government ministries. They were state-owned institutions and merely provided working capital and credit for projects approved by the planning authorities. There was only one financial asset, money, and enterprises obtained funds through their own internal accumulation, subsidies from the government, or bank credits. Central control was maintained by taxing away a sufficient amount of internal funds to ensure that the enterprises would have to rely on credit. Governments used subsidies and arbitrary and often confiscatory taxes to redistribute income from successful to failing enterprises to prevent the failures from going out of business. Given the arbitrary structure of relative prices, profit or loss could not be used as an indicator of performance.

One notable legacy of the old system is the lack of a legal system to protect property rights and enforce contracts between economic agents.[6] Administrative rules and procedures in a highly hierarchical bureaucracy supplanted laws and the market. Today, there is no shortage of laws, but they mean little because the countries have no tradition of abiding by them or enforcing them, and they undergo continuous modification in response to shifting political power. The lack of respect for the sanctity of laws governing commerce, contracts, and property rights remains a large barrier to the expansion of the private sector and, specifically, to inflows of foreign capital.

Another legacy was the pervasive state ownership of production facilities and natural resources. Therefore extraordinarily little private wealth is available to finance a transition to privately owned enterprises, and the method of moving to private ownership has proved to be one of the most divisive and difficult aspects of the transition process.

Foreign Trade and Comparative Advantage

Another characteristic of the centrally planned economies was their isolation from the global economy, which stemmed from their emphasis on economic self-sufficiency for the bloc as a whole. Indeed, their participation in the global trading system that developed after World War II was minimal. In 1985 Western Europe's trade with the Soviet bloc amounted to $72 billion, or only 5 percent of its total trade volume.[7] In addition, the state monopoly over trade was used to isolate the structure of domestic prices from the prices on world markets. Export goods were purchased from enterprises at domestic prices, and all foreign exchange was rebated to the government. Meanwhile, the domestic prices of imports were based on the prices of comparable domestic products, rather than on their costs.

One result of this system was that foreign trade had no influence on the incentives individual enterprises faced, since they were completely

6. Litwack (1991).
7. UN Economic Commission for Europe (1989, appendix tables 1, 6, and 7).

isolated from the global market. Not only did the prices they paid or received not reflect those of the world market, but they were unprepared to deal with customers or to redesign products as needed to sell abroad.

The centrally planned economies of Eastern Europe and the Soviet Union developed their own trading network, the Council for Mutual Economic Assistance (CMEA). They conducted trade via government-to-government bilateral agreements, supposedly at "world prices." The unit of account was the "transferable ruble," and although it was used for all CMEA transactions, it never became an instrument of multilateral clearing among the members. The main reason was that the above-mentioned world prices were determined in each bilateral agreement at the discretion of the negotiators and therefore had no clear and uniform value in any other context. Thus there were few multilateral agreements, and third-party clearing was rare.

In general, the CMEA terms of trade favored the East European partners and served as a means of providing subsidies for these countries. The prices charged for Soviet exports, mostly energy and other raw materials, were either below or near world prices, whereas the prices for consumer goods and machinery from Central Europe were significantly inflated.[8] CMEA trade was also attractive to the other countries because it used a soft currency and involved goods that could not be sold on world markets.

Despite the archaic system of CMEA trade, the level of exports and imports, inclusive of CMEA trade, was comparable to trade levels of the West. Soviet imports in the late 1980s, for example, represented about 12 percent of GNP, a figure comparable to that for the United States.[9] Because of the nature of the planning system, these countries were actually more dependent on trade than many Western economies. Soviet planners, in particular, used imports from other CMEA countries in lieu of domestic production of entire lines of products, since competitive imports were viewed as wasteful. Thus the collapse of the system in the 1990s was extremely disruptive because of the

8. Formally, prices for CMEA trade were determined on the basis of five-year averages of world prices. This rule was changed for energy after the 1973 energy crisis, whereupon prices were adjusted more rapidly. As a result, during the 1980s energy prices to some CMEA countries exceeded world prices; but they still paid with exports, the prices of which were far above those of equivalent products in the West.

9. Hewett and Gaddy (1992, p. 16).

Table 1-1. *Geographical Structure of Trade, Socialist Economies, 1989*
Percent of total

	Trading partner				
Country	Central Europe[a]	Soviet Union	Developed market economies	Developing economies	Total
Bulgaria	12.5	41.7	27.5	16.1	100
Czechoslovakia	21.0	26.2	37.6	8.9	100
Hungary	16.5	23.6	46.2	7.8	100
Poland	16.5	22.9	44.9	7.5	100
Romania	12.6	18.5	32.5	31.3	100
Soviet Union	25.4	n.a.	45.9	21.5	100

Source: United Nations, Economic Commission for Europe (1992, pp. 51–52).

Note: Based on average values of exports and imports using standardized ruble-dollar cross rates of exchange. Components do not add to 100 because of exclusion of trade with some formerly socialist economies.

a. Includes the former German Democratic Republic.

lack of alternative sources of supply for previously imported critical materials and equipment, or markets for exports.

The geographical distribution of trade of the major CMEA countries in 1989 is given in table 1-1.[10] Although the degree of dependency on CMEA trade varied greatly, it averaged nearly half of the total. It was actually quite low for the Soviet Union, at 25 percent of its total trade. Trade with the West was heavily dominated by trade with Western Europe, and the volume of trade with the United States and Japan was trivial. The situation in China before the reforms of the 1980s reflected a much lower level of dependency on other socialist economies—it was not a member of the CMEA—and a more diversified geographical pattern of trade with the rest of the world (see table 2-3).

Under the socialist system and its growth strategy, the composition of production and the pattern of comparative advantage differed from

10. Measures of trade are extremely variable because of the difficulties of valuing trade in the transferable ruble. Here we have focused on statistics from the Economic Commission for Europe because of its efforts to convert nonconvertible currency trade at realistic exchange rates. Later, in examining trade developments in the 1990–93 period, we rely on information from *Direction of Trade Statistics,* published by the International Monetary Fund.

that of most industrial and developing economies.[11] These differences were most pronounced for the industrialized countries of Central Europe and the Soviet Union. They were less significant for China, which was a largely agricultural and very poor country when it began its reforms.

The collectivization of agriculture at the outset of the socialist revolution, which was intended to free up resources for rapid industrialization, eliminated a comparative advantage in food and agricultural products, and with it, most food exports, at least exports outside the socialist bloc. The Central European region, a net exporter of food before World War II, rapidly became a net importer. This was especially the case in the Soviet Union, where relative productivity in agriculture deteriorated rapidly; even heavy investments in fertilizers and equipment during the 1970s and 1980s did not produce the expected benefits. Highly subsidized food prices (for bread, meat, and dairy products) increased demand and hence imports.

In industry there was a strong bias in favor of heavy industry (metallurgy, machinery, industrial construction) and against consumer goods and services. Investment and research and development concentrated on heavy industry and defense. For a long period, the population had to make do with few material goods: the old regime restricted the production of automotive products for private use, provided only limited housing, and allowed almost no imports of consumer goods. The development of services was constrained by the absence of markets, the bias against private consumption, and the Marxian doctrine that services were nonproductive. The authoritarian regime also restricted tourism, the media, and other information services.

With so much emphasis on the metalworking and machine-building industries, including defense, the regime might have been expected to create a comparative advantage in the products of these industries, at least in the less sophisticated, capital- and resource-intensive types. Yet trade in such goods took place mostly within the socialist bloc,

---

11. In what follows we refer to several theories on the evolution of comparative advantage as part of the process of economic growth: those of Hecksher-Ohlin; Chenery and Syrquin (1975); Linder (1961); Porter (1990). The relevant elements of the socialist system and growth strategy are incorporated together to save space. For a detailed analysis of the pattern of trade under the old regime see Collins and Rodrik (1991); Ofer (1991); Beenstock (1992).

although arms and some machinery were exported to developing countries, but there were almost no such exports to industrialized market economies. This was due to the functional autarky mentioned above, the general systemic weakness of centrally planned economies in the indigenous development of R&D, and the concentration of most R&D on military needs.

Many factors combined to prevent these economies from enjoying the wave of technological advances in computer technology and applications, communications, electronics and electronic control, data processing and information management and dissemination, and the development of new materials. Most of these are process innovations that can be applied to a broad range of industries but are very difficult to introduce in a centrally planned system, where tasks are assigned to individual product-oriented ministries. Other inhibiting factors were the weak R&D, the political control over information, and possibly also the timing: the fact that the advances were taking place at a time when the system was already in decline.

The economies in transition are clearly lagging behind the world economy in both product and process technology, and they will have to build trade relations on some factor advantage, such as natural resources (which are plentiful in Russia) or cheap semiskilled labor (which is abundant in Central Europe), concentrating on simple processed products and widely available technologies for some time.[12] Such exports are subject to fierce competition and are often limited by trade barriers (in agriculture and food; in steel, aluminum, and other metals; and in textiles).[13]

On the demand side, there is a radical shift in composition, both among the leading categories of end uses—where the move has been away from investment and military production and toward consumption—and within each of the these categories. Here, too, there is an incompatibility between East and West that encompasses the structure, quality, and assortment of both producer and consumer goods. This creates difficulties not only for domestic producers seeking buyers in the West but also for those trying to compete in the internal markets of former centrally planned economies: the domestic Eastern consumers seem to prefer Western goods even with high price premiums.

12. Russia may be an exception in that, with its extensive natural resources, it can base a long-term strategy on this stage, as is discussed more fully below.

13. See, for example, Ostry (1993); Dyker (1993a); Hindley (1993).

In summary, the restructuring of production in Central Europe and the former Soviet Union is more complex than the classical liberalization of a developing economy following a period of import substitution: the industrial sector is much larger, the required restructuring is more radical, and the technologies less compatible. And it is necessary to create from scratch an entire market and service infrastructure.[14] Only part of the old industrial base and specialization can be adapted to the new conditions. Western technology is now superior both in production processes and in the variety and quality of products, the composition of internal demand is completely different, and relative prices have a new structure. In most cases, the East European technologies are not only inferior to but also incompatible with their counterparts in parallel lines of production in the West. This difference in technological bases reduces the potential for intraindustry trade.[15]

China began its reforms with a considerable advantage in this regard. Its industrial sector was not overdeveloped and most of its population was still employed in agriculture. Thus economic liberalization could more quickly translate into increased levels of output, and it did not face the same immediate need to restructure the industrial sector.

Basic Elements of an Economic Reform Program

The process of economic transition requires simultaneous actions in a host of different areas that are all interrelated, and it has proved very difficult to determine the order in which these actions should take place. What is unique about economic reform in centrally planned economies is the scale of the required change. To add to the complexity of the task, the legacy of the prior system of central planning does not provide a framework for thinking about economic problems and dealing with them from a market perspective. Moreover, the economic change is occurring in a new political environment

14. On the structure of comparative advantage of the East European countries, and on prospects of its development, see a detailed analysis by Collins and Rodrik (1991, chaps. 2 and 4).

15. The importance for trade of similar technology bases is demonstrated in Linder (1961); Porter (1990).

in which fragile democracies are struggling to establish a political framework for making and implementing decisions.

The initial thrust of the reforms in Central Europe and the former Soviet Union was to simply relax the administrative controls of central planning. Markets would simply spring up of their own accord within a decentralized system with liberalized prices. Particularly in the former Soviet Union, the reformers resembled anarchists in their eagerness to destroy the old system, but they failed to agree on the structures that would replace it. What they precipitated was not reform but chaos and collapse, because the institutions needed to coordinate markets were not there. The reformers have learned that the government must play a more active role than previously believed to create those institutions.

Although various Central European countries experimented with economic reform before 1990, those partial reform efforts appear to have had little positive effect on economic growth.[16] The fact that any such effort must have both an internal and external dimension is illustrated by the attempts of several Central European countries to liberalize the foreign trade sector in the 1980s: their programs were ineffective because they neglected to undertake a similar liberalization of the domestic economy. The mismatch between the domestic and foreign price structure continued to create highly perverse incentives, and the system remained too inflexible to ensure that firms would have the inputs to support changing levels of export activity.

Some analysts have concluded that gradual reform will not work, that what is needed is a drastic and complete overhaul of the prior system, and that its institutions should be immediately replaced with completely new ones. But historical experience provides no evidence of the success of that approach. To a large extent, the reformers are operating in the dark: they know where they want to go, but they have no blueprint of the precise sequence of reforms that will get them there. There is, however, agreement on the broad agenda of reform: price liberalization, privatization, the establishment of commercial law, the establishment of a system of financial intermediation, macroeconomic stabilization, and reform of the foreign trade system.[17]

16. Beenstock (1992). The author makes the point that liberal communism should not be confused with capitalism, and experiments with the former suggest little about the success of the latter.

17. There are several other areas of a comprehensive reform program, such as labor market institutions and fiscal reform, that we do not address.

Price Liberalization

The first prerequisite of an efficient market economy is a rational set of prices that can be used to signal the appropriate allocation of resources. Prices played no such allocative function under the old system. Prices must be freely determined in line with underlying resource costs before world markets will open up to the products of the transitional economies. One key requirement of membership in the General Agreement on Tariffs and Trade (GATT) is that there be a clear link between international and domestic prices, and that trade be regulated through tariffs rather than administrative controls. Price liberalization is critical to several other aspects of the reform process. The government cannot impose hard budget constraints on enterprises, cut off their subsidy payments, and force unprofitable firms to close unless they are operating with prices that reflect real resource costs. Furthermore, enterprises cannot be privately owned or controlled unless markets are opened. Hungary and Poland experimented with price reform in previous decades, but price reform is not price liberalization. Their supposedly free prices remained subject to extensive administrative intervention and revision of the rules.

All of the current reform programs began with some degree of price liberalization. This turned out to be a complicated process because of the extreme monopolization that had developed in the leading sectors of these economies, and their lack of the normal coordinating institutions of markets.[18] Although the liberalization soon eliminated shortages and the queues for basic necessities, in combination with an initial overhang of excess money balances, it caused a sharp rise in aggregate inflation and thwarted efforts to maintain macroeconomic stability.

Price liberalization worked best at the retail level, where consumers were faced with hard budget constraints. It has been less successful at the wholesale level because budget constraints are not binding on state enterprises and many firms continue to enjoy strong monopoly

18. An example is provided by the Polish price liberalization of 1990, which resulted in much higher retail food prices combined with a severe financial squeeze on private farmers. That abnormality was a result of monopoly control on the wholesale and retail food distribution system on the demand side, and higher interest rates and sharp increases in fertilizer prices that accompanied the reduction of government subsidies on the supply side. In time, that problem was resolved as the farmers circumvented the distribution system to bring their products directly to the city.

power. This is particularly evident in Russia, where the prices of producer goods in manufacturing rose more than those for consumer goods, and wholesale prices rose more than retail prices. Efforts to break up monopolies and promote competition have thus far been limited, and reforms in the financial sector have failed to impose hard budget constraints on the larger enterprises. The inflation pressures precipitated by price liberalization and the initial devaluation of the exchange rate required restrictive macroeconomic policies that contributed to the decline in output.

Price liberalization has been most successful in the major Central European countries. For the most part, prices there now reflect underlying costs and demand and supply conditions. Problems, as discussed more fully in later sections, have arisen in the interaction of price reform with trade liberalization and exchange rate determination. Imported goods, particularly capital equipment, are extremely expensive in relation to domestically priced labor, pushing these economies toward the most extreme form of labor-intensive production techniques. The overall result is a large change in relative prices that is necessitating a larger than anticipated restructuring of industry.

The process is particularly incomplete in the former Soviet Union, where many key material prices, notably energy, remain subject to control, and the magnitude and speed of the relative price changes severely distorted trade among regions and republics. During 1994, direct price controls on energy products were removed, but export quotas and similar quantitative restrictions led to the same result. The distortion of domestic prices in relation to the global market was larger than in Central Europe, and the collapse of exchange rates greatly affected efforts to establish a rational structure of relative prices.

Privatization

In the early stages of reform, privatization was considered the salvation of the transitional economies. It was expected to bring in substantial public revenues and quickly transform the economies into a market-based system. It would rapidly create a strong entrepreneurial class, change socioeconomic attitudes, and provide a means of rebalancing political power between the public and private sectors.

The reality is that privatization of the large enterprises has been moving very slowly, has become a highly controversial political issue, and is unlikely to generate significant public revenue. The continuing debate over privatization and the impossibility of implementing a rational plan in a short time has left many state-owned enterprises in limbo with no clear idea of the steps that they should take to become more efficient.

The critical issue in privatization is not private ownership, but how to introduce an effective system of controlling and governing the enterprises. Given the lack of private wealth, these countries cannot privatize everything unless it is simply given away. Foreign investment might be seen as a source of financing for privatization, but it has been limited by concerns about giving away national resources.[19] Furthermore, foreign investors have often sought to limit competition in the domestic market as a condition of their entry. The whole process is further encumbered by the lack of information about the potential value of the enterprises in an economy undergoing rapid structural change, and public concerns about the fairness of any privatization scheme. To its advocates, privatization is an important means of dismantling the old system and ensuring that the reform process will not be reversed. It is also an important means of breaking the political link between the government and the enterprises.[20] Critics have argued that the privatization of the large firms should be delayed pending restructuring, demonopolization, and the creation of an infrastructure that could support the enterprises, particularly a functioning financial system. They have tended to put greater emphasis on the issue of effective control and competition.

The privatization schemes have relied on the mass dispersal of ownership through vouchers or the creation of investment funds, the shares of which are owned by the general public. These programs could be implemented quickly, but the initial values assigned to the enterprises were more or less random, and they may do little to establish strong governance. Widely dispersed groups of owners are primarily interested in developing equity markets in which they can trade shares, rather than in intervening to restructure troubled enter-

19. Hungary, with a longer tradition of involvement with foreign firms, has encouraged them to participate in its privatization program. About 5 percent of GDP is produced within foreign-owned firms.

20. Boycko, Shleifer, and Vishny (1993); Blanchard and others (1991).

prises. Corporations in which no one shareholder has the incentive to monitor or control the operation are experiencing severe free-rider problems. That dispersed shareholders could exercise effective control seems particularly unlikely in view of the extreme economic concentration that was the starting point of the transition and the strong tradition of bureaucratic control in these countries.[21] Furthermore, few of them have a functioning financial market that could impose discipline or finance any significant restructuring.

Surprisingly, the process of privatizing the large enterprises has actually gone the furthest in Russia, where the initiative has shifted from the central government to the enterprises themselves. It has been aided by the extreme distrust of the central government and a general policy of reform from the bottom up. The old system of state orders has collapsed, and with the reduction of subsidies, the government also lost its leverage over what had become largely autonomous state enterprises. Privatization was a formal recognition of that autonomous status. Many firms have been privatized, but an examination of the prices indicates that they are being virtually given away, not sold. As already mentioned, the government has issued marketable vouchers that are then used to purchase shares in firms in public auctions. Existing management and workers, however, have been given sufficient shares to provide them with majority control. The low prices reflect the strong degree of insider control, as well as the extreme economic, institutional, and political uncertainty surrounding the privatizations.[22] Since no effort was made to clean up the balance sheet of old credits and debits with other enterprises and the banks before privatization, the important issue of financial discipline remains unresolved.[23]

Another problem is that few of the large state enterprises are likely to have a substantial net economic value. Even in the West, there are few examples of the successful transformation of large inefficient state

21. Although corporate share ownership is widespread in the United States and Great Britain, the mechanisms of corporate governance through takeovers and management of the enterprise in the sole interests of the stockholders in unlikely to work in the economies in transition, which have a completely different tradition. It may take a long time for outside groups of stockholders to emerge with sufficient ownership to seize control. Thus the enterprises would continue to be controlled by insiders.

22. Further details are provided in Boycko, Shleifer, and Vishny (1993).

23. Old debt is less of a problem in Russia, where an explosive rate of inflation has destroyed its real value.

enterprises into strong private corporations. In effect, a significant number of the old enterprises are simply vast unemployment insurance funds, using their existing capital stock to produce some products that will cover a portion of the wage cost of a slowly shrinking pool of workers.

As is so evident in China, future growth will come from the creation and expansion of new firms, not the transformation of old enterprises. China has not attempted to privatize the existing large state enterprises but has focused instead on the development of new nonstate enterprises. In fact, the growth of the Chinese economy has been overwhelmingly the result of the development of this new semi-private sector rather than the growth of the existing firms. Yet there is some evidence that the state enterprises have improved their performance, gradually learning to operate with tightening market constraints and changed incentives; at least in the short run, these gains can be achieved without privatization.[24] In Central Europe and the former Soviet Union, however, these enterprises account for a far more important share of total production and employment. These countries cannot afford to waste the capital invested in them, and they cannot afford the unemployment consequences of being allowed to fail.

Most of the transitional economies have made rapid progress in creating a private sector based on small enterprises. These firms are concentrated in retail trade and services, sectors that were severely repressed under the old regime. The transfer to private ownership was relatively easy to accomplish by turning the enterprise over to its workers and leasing the premises. There has also been a rapid expansion of new small enterprises, but again they are concentrated in services and trade where the need for capital, which is in scarce supply, is low.

Despite the delays, the simple transfer of ownership will turn out to be the easy part of the privatization process. The hard part is to create an institutional framework that is supportive of private enterprise and to ensure that management emerges as an advocate of the preservation of capital. In China, local governments often serve as the effective

---

24. The performance of the state-operated enterprises in China is discussed more fully in a later section. Pinto, Belka, and Krajewski (1993) provide evidence of some significant restructuring of the Polish state enterprises.

entrepreneurs, initiating new enterprises and promoting the development of markets. Township governments play a central role in circumventing the old institutions. Such a role has yet to emerge in Russia. Instead, local officials there tend to resist change and try to maintain their control, in many cases by extracting bribes. China also benefits enormously from the financial and technical assistance of overseas Chinese, something unavailable in Russia.

With the notable exception of China, the transitional economies have been slow to create a stable legal and institutional framework for attracting private capital from abroad. China also demonstrates that privatization of the existing enterprises is not a precondition to the rapid expansion of trade. It established special trade zones that allowed foreign firms to take advantage of a large pool of inexpensive labor without being encumbered by the rigidities of the system of state-owned enterprises.

Development of a Financial System

All of the formerly centrally planned economies are plagued by extremely repressed financial systems. Under the prior system of bureaucratic control, the financial system played no allocative role in distributing savings to the most efficient investment projects. More important, it had no means of disciplining firms to ensure that scarce capital was used efficiently. A single institution provided the services of both a central bank and a commercial bank. Loans were made with no particular consideration of the ability to repay, and the notion of bad loans was a somewhat alien concept. Other financial institutions existed, but they had narrowly prescribed functions such as financing foreign trade, providing credits for housing and agriculture, and serving the needs of households. The passive role of the bank in supplying credit was a principal factor behind the pervasive shortages in most markets. Investment decisions were made and financed through the government ministries, and thus the financial system played no part in the evaluation of projects.

An efficient financial system cannot be created overnight, if for no other reason than the degree of expertise it requires in its loan officers, accounting standards, and regulatory system. Thus, the goals of reform in the financial sector must be limited, with a strong focus on basic functions. That means the emphasis must be on developing a strong and closely supervised banking system. Despite the infatuation with equity and bond markets in public discussions of the reforms, these auction-type markets can easily become a source of destabilizing speculation in the early stages of the reform process, when information about enterprises is severely limited.

Commercial banks have a critical role to play in the early stages of the reform process. On one hand, they are the essential component of a financial intermediation system that channels funds from savers to investors. Capital is quickly emerging as the major restriction on the conversion of industry in these economies, and the mobilization and efficient allocation of savings will have a strong influence on future growth prospects. On the other hand, the industrial enterprises cannot be converted to private firms with strong management discipline in a short period of time. Thus, even more than in the West, these economies need a set of institutions that will serve to discipline the enterprises and force them to conserve scarce capital. Furthermore, a strong regulatory system will be needed to enforce a realistic evaluation of loans, capital adequacy, and limits to excessive risk exposure.

Thus far, efforts to reform the financial system have produced meager results. If anything, they have caused new, even more serious problems. One of the first steps has been to create a two-tier banking system in which the functions of the central bank and commercial banks are separated.[25] In several countries that reform has given rise to a relatively independent central bank that has successfully shifted from direct to indirect control over credit. However, the second tier was created by simply transferring existing loans of the prior monobank to new state-owned commercial banks. A very large proportion of those loans were nonperforming, which means that the new banks were bankrupt from the beginning in the sense that their own capital position was negative.[26]

Because of the rudimentary nature of the financial system, standard macroeconomic stabilization measures can only go so far. The efforts of the central bank to control aggregate credit have been

25. A two-tier banking system was created as early as 1985 in Hungary and 1987 in Poland, and more recently in Russia.

26. The proportion of nonperforming loans is estimated to be 25 percent of total debt or more in the stronger Eastern European economies and even higher in Russia. This may be less of a problem in Russia, however, where any real value of the existing loans has been eroded by inflation.

subverted by the growth of interenterprise credit in which a firm simply delays payment of debts to other enterprises. The creditor enterprises cover the shortfall by drawing down deposits with the banks, reducing their tax payments, or failing to repay outstanding loans to the banks. The banks cannot afford to pursue bankruptcy proceedings against these borrowers since a write-down of the loan would reveal their own insolvency. In fact, they often capitalize delinquent loan repayments, treating them like a new loan. Thus insolvent banks make loans to insolvent enterprises, with the central bank providing the credit to prevent the system's collapse. There are private banks; but they are generally undercapitalized and weakly supervised.

Without intervention, aggregate credit restraint falls most heavily on the private sector, as happened in China in 1989 and Poland in 1990. The authorities are urged to establish high real interest rates as part of credit restraint, but the weakest state firms continue to borrow even at prohibitively high interest rates since the alternative is bankruptcy. They simply roll over unpaid interest in new credit as a means of delaying the day of reckoning. This tendency of high real interest rates to result in excessive risk taking, rather than restraint, has been documented as a frequent occurrence in situations of financial crisis in other economies.[27] At the same time, some countries, such as Russia, have failed to maintain the minimum standard of a positive real interest rate and have thereby destroyed incentives to hold savings in a financial form.

The financial sector is an area in which the active participation of foreign institutions offers significant advantages. They would bring in skilled management and technology. They would also provide an immediate link to international capital markets and a means of assisting domestic firms with foreign transactions. Such institutions would also attract foreign investors. Their participation does involve some risks, however. Their presence brings into focus the issue of the currency denomination of domestic loans and deposits and raises questions about who will have control over external capital account transactions: will domestic firms and individuals be allowed to undertake financial transactions in foreign currencies? If so, these activities will significantly alter the costs and risks to the domestic economy of exchange rate changes. Financial markets in the transitional econo-

27. McKinnon (1991, particularly chap. 7).

mies tend to be very thin and volatile and are easily influenced by large-scale financial transactions of a few institutions. To date, the involvement of foreign financial institutions is restricted in many countries by fears of external economic and political domination and by the desire of domestic banks to limit competition.

Macroeconomic Stabilization

In the early stages of the reform process, the transitional economies differed greatly in their need for macroeconomic stabilization. China opted for gradual reform and therefore continued to exercise central control over the macroeconomy. Although it has had periodic problems with excessive demand and inflation, the government has maintained a reasonable degree of control over fiscal and monetary policy. In Russia, however, both fiscal and monetary policy spun out of control. Failing to make a sharp political break with the past, as did most of the Central European countries, Russia got caught up in a struggle for control between those calling for radical economic reform and conservatives. It also faced numerous problems associated with the breakup of the former Soviet Union. Even in Central Europe, where new governments came to power to manage the reform process, initial conditions varied greatly. Poland began 1990 with hyperinflation and massive fiscal-monetary imbalances. It had to apply severe shock therapy to address those distortions. Although Hungary and Czechoslovakia began with relatively benign macroeconomic situations, Hungary was faced with an extremely large foreign debt.

Structural problems in the fiscal and financial systems of all these countries sharply differentiate their conduct of stabilization policy from that of Western market economies. Economic reform brings with it a sharp decline in government revenues and almost inevitably a fiscal crisis.[28] All of the transitional countries had outdated fiscal systems that relied heavily on the surpluses of state enterprises and turnover taxes to finance the state budget. Reform brought a collapse of state enterprise profits, and the governments had no effective mechanism for collecting taxes from the newly emerging private sec-

28. Government revenues declined by about 10 percent of GDP in China during the 1980s to their current share near 20 percent. In the 1990s, state revenues in the Eastern European economies have fallen by about 5 percentage points, but are still above 30 percent of GDP. The drop in the CIS has been even more rapid (World Bank, 1994b).

tor. On the expenditure side, they achieved some immediate gains through the reduction of subsidies to state enterprises; but they had to create new social safety net programs, which are now becoming very expensive. Additional burdens are imposed by the need to transfer responsibilities for some services, such as health, education, and housing, from the enterprises to the government. This transfer was essential for preparing the state-owned enterprises for privatization. As in similar crises elsewhere, investments in an already dilapidated public infrastructure declined sharply in the early stages of transition in both Central Europe and the republics of the former Soviet Union.

Furthermore, because no sharp line is drawn between the general government budget and a more inclusive fiscal measure that incorporates the government enterprises, the meaning of the budget deficit from a stabilization perspective is distorted. For example, if subsidies are excluded from the budget, but picked up by the central bank in the form of credit to failing enterprises, little has been accomplished. Given the high level of unemployment compensation, a focus on budget costs leads the government to encourage firms to hoard workers. Yet the enterprise costs emerge in lost tax revenues, excessive borrowing, and delayed restructuring. These problems often lead fiscal experts to suggest that stabilization policy focus on monetary questions, so as not to impinge on the fiscal reforms.

In the larger economies fiscal federalism has also created significant problems since, under the old system, all revenues flowed from the center. With reform, the central governments have shifted expenditure functions onto lower levels without a similar transfer of tax revenues. As a result, local governments have had to intervene to prevent the transfer of local enterprise taxes to the central government.[29]

Like other institutional reforms, the modernization of the tax system will proceed slowly because it will take time to develop the expertise and accounting systems required for efficient tax collection. The system will gradually have to replace profit taxes with value added taxes. At the beginning of the reform process, profit tax revenues in the Central European economies were roughly 10–15 percent of GDP compared with an average of 3 percent in the countries of the Organization for Economic Cooperation and Development (OECD).[30] The new

29. Wallich (1992).
30. Tanzi (1993a, table 1).

tax system cannot simply copy from the industrial countries, however, because those systems are too complex for the transitional economies in their present state. Individual income taxes are therefore unlikely to be a major source of revenue in the near future. Excise and import duties are likely to provide much of the transitional funding. Employ-ment taxes are used to finance social programs, but those tax rates are already very high, in part as a result of the very low wages in many enterprises, in which social expenditures rather than wages provide a significant portion of workers' compensation. At the same time, the movement of workers to an untaxed, or informal, private sector is eroding the tax base. Even with tax reform, these economies will need to reduce expenditures, which are far beyond the 25–30 percent of GDP that their tax systems might be capable of generating on the revenue side. This will be difficult now that unemployment is beginning to rise.

Yet equally strong arguments can be made that stabilization policy has relied too heavily on monetary restraint. Consequently, a conflict has arisen between the advocates of strong credit restraints to stabilize the macroeconomy in the short run and those who would finance the longer-term restructuring of potentially efficient enterprises. Even under ideal circumstances it is not easy to tell when the extension of credit is a good risk for the future. It is particularly difficult in the midst of the massive restructuring now taking place in these econo-mies. Extreme credit restraint will curb demand and impose price stability, but on the supply side it may also lead to premature closures and forgone investments.[31]

Similar connections exist between stabilization policy and adjust-ments of the exchange rate. Several of the transitional economies are heavily indebted. Many economists therefore suggest the nominal exchange rate should be the primary policy indicator and should be used to establish the credibility of the stabilization program. Such an emphasis on a target for the nominal exchange rate, however, may lead to an overvaluation of the real exchange rate and limit the development of an export sector; but efforts to correct it might also reduce credibility in the battle against inflation.

Finally, the economies in transition will face serious problems as they try to restrain wage increases in the pursuit of price stability. Given the weak management of enterprises, the lack of a strong

31. Calvo and Coricelli (1993).

incentive to conserve capital, and expropriatory tax rates on profits, they are unlikely to resist wage increases. Despite the weak record of incomes policies in other countries, these economies are often urged to develop some direct means of wage restraint in the state enterprises during the transitional period.[32]

Foreign Sector Liberalization

An early opening of the external sector has generally been viewed as critical to the reform process. In the initial stages of price liberalization, it was thought that the global market would provide the most relevant guide to a rational price structure. Foreign competition was also viewed as the simplest way to introduce competition into a heavily cartelized domestic market. A convertible currency and free trade would assist in evaluating the competitiveness of state enterprises. Furthermore, a convertible currency would provide an important guide, or nominal anchor, for the conduct of domestic stabilization policy. Some observers also saw convertible currencies as the only effective means of restoring trade among the countries of the Council for Mutual Economic Assistance (known informally as COMECON), which collapsed in 1991.

Although this rapid opening was encouraged by Western advisers, it is sometimes forgotten that the industrial countries followed a rather different strategy in formulating their own trade policies, in that they spread tariff reduction and the move to convertible currencies over several decades. The European economies and Japan maintained strong controls on capital inflows and outflows for many years and often used trade policy to guide the development of domestic industries.

For the economies in transition, foreign sector liberalization represented a major change from the previous state monopoly over foreign trade: it meant replacing administrative controls with indirect regulation through a unification of the exchange rate and the establishment of a tariff structure; establishing links with international organizations such as GATT, the International Monetary Fund, and the World Bank, which most of these countries had previously shunned; and creating a convertible currency. All of these measures are the antith-

32. Blanchard and others (1991).

esis of the old practices, which isolated the domestic economy from global economic forces.

TRADE POLICY. The transitional economies have drastically changed the structure of their foreign trade system. Most have virtually eliminated the prior state monopoly over trade. In Central Europe and the states of the former Soviet Union, individual firms are now allowed to engage in foreign trade. The need to combine trade liberalization with the continuation of substantial domestic price controls has led China to follow a more complex process of expanding the number of foreign trade corporations and gradually reducing the restrictions on their activities. In the republics of the former Soviet Union, the state monopoly over trade is limited to a few products. Export licensing is restricted to products subject to domestic price controls, where the purpose is to prevent the reexport of subsidized items, and most countries have introduced liberalized import licensing.

Tariff schedules played no practical role under central planning. Some Central European economies introduced official tariff schedules when they joined GATT, but their structure was arbitrary before domestic price liberalization.[33] Yet a key principle of GATT is that there should be a clear connection between domestic and international prices and that trade should be regulated through tariffs rather than quotas, licensing, or other administrative devices. At the aggregate level, tariffs are highly substitutable for exchange rate policy in determining the average level of protection afforded domestic producers. The principal argument for a high average tariff is that it can contribute to government revenues during the time that the domestic revenue system is still inefficient and underdeveloped.

A more significant concern is the extent of differentiation of the tariff structure, since a high tariff may unduly delay restructuring of the more protected industries. Industries may differ significantly in the time they take to restructure, with the result that too rapid an opening may destroy domestic enterprises that could be competitive with the international market in time. This is a variant of the infant-industry argument on behalf of industries with the potential to develop dynamic comparative advantage through restructuring. A highly differentiated tariff schedule can also create enforcement prob-

---

33. The four largest Eastern European countries were members of GATT, but they operated under special provisions.

lems as importers reclassify goods into the more advantageous categories: in practice, most of the economies in transition have had to build the customs system from scratch.[34]

EXCHANGE RATE POLICY AND CONVERTIBILITY. Exchange rate reform involved particularly large changes because the national currencies of the centrally planned economies were not convertible for the most part, and they maintained multiple exchange rates for different kinds of products and different geographical regions. The first reforms concentrated on unifying the multiple rates, establishing an exchange rate regime, and introducing a degree of convertibility. In Central Europe and Russia the rates were unified quickly but conflicting objectives made it difficult to settle on a level for the new single rate. On one hand, a low exchange rate would promote the rapid growth of exports and provide domestic industries with some protection from international competition in the restructuring. Also, most of the transitional economies had limited foreign exchange reserves and had to avoid balance of payments problems. On the other hand, a large devaluation would intensify the inflationary pressures on the domestic economy, through a large surge in the price of imported goods. China maintained a dual exchange rate system until 1994.

The economies also had to choose a specific exchange rate regime: a fixed rate, a floating rate, or a crawling peg. A fixed rate is generally advocated as part of a domestic stabilization program because it limits the flexibility of domestic fiscal and monetary policy and makes more credible the government's commitment to restraining inflation pressures, by providing a nominal anchor for judging day-to-day monetary policy. It also permits global prices to be the basis for a new domestic price structure. If the government fails to achieve reasonable price stability, however, a fixed rate can quickly lead to overvaluation of the real rate and a loss of competitiveness for the tradable goods sector. Furthermore, if inflation is insensitive to market conditions, the effort to hold the exchange rate can exert an excessive degree of restraint on the domestic economy.

A flexible rate relieves the government of the need to worry about exchange rate reserves; and, because it is determined by the demand

---

34. Accession to GATT also generally means that a country's tariff structure is bound by the agreement and can only be changed through consultation. At present, most of the transitional economies have only observer status or limited accession. The exceptions are the Czech Republic and Hungary, the majority of whose tariffs are bound.

and supply for foreign currencies, the rate is more likely to be supportive of trade expansion. The risk in this case is that flexibility may turn into excessive volatility, and repeated depreciations may lead to an inflationary spiral. A crawling peg—under which the exchange rate is allowed to float within a predetermined band, which can be adjusted in line with the past or anticipated inflation differential with trading partners—is often proposed as a compromise strategy.

Convertibility refers to the freedom to convert between national and foreign currencies at a legal exchange rate for international transactions. There are degrees of convertibility. Current account convertibility, as embodied in the IMF Articles of Agreement, refers to the removal of restrictions on foreign currency exchange for purposes of settling transactions involving the purchase of goods and services, the payment of interest, or the repatriation of profits. Full convertibility extends this principle to the purchase and sale of assets, which is known as capital account convertibility. Although the standard definitions of convertibility distinguish among the purposes of the transactions (capital versus current account transactions), within the transitional economies it is also common to distinguish among the parties to the transaction. Thus, they take internal convertibility to mean allowing residents to make exchanges between domestic and foreign currencies while excluding foreigners.[35]

Generally, the transitional economies have been encouraged to move quickly toward current account convertibility but to take their time in removing restrictions on capital flows. Capital account convertibility raises the risk of instability from capital flight or speculation in thin currency markets and the tremendous uncertainty associated with the transition. Many of these countries lack the reserves required to counter speculative pressures, particularly if they have chosen a fixed exchange rate as part of their domestic stabilization program. In order to attract foreign investors, current account convertibility is usually extended to include capital repatriation for direct foreign investment.

There is also considerable historical evidence that the timing of external liberalization is of vast importance. Many countries that attempted to liberalize foreign financial transactions early in their reform process experienced severe crises in their foreign exchange

---

35. Williamson (1991).

markets and financial collapse. Thus countries are normally urged to postpone capital account liberalization until a strong trade system has been established and they have developed a stable domestic financial market. Furthermore, current account liberalization cannot precede domestic price liberalization without creating extreme problems of arbitrage between a distorted domestic price structure and world market prices.[36]

Internal convertibility has taken on considerable importance in the transitional economies of Central Europe and the former Soviet Union as a symbol of reduced government control. In practice it has applied to foreign exchange accounts of households and not enterprises. Such accounts might be justified if the range of investment alternatives in which households could seek protection against inflation risks (such as real estate and commodities) were still limited. Although the potential for shifting into dollar accounts can be said to add greater discipline to government anti-inflation programs, it increases the risk of financial instability if the shift of funds into such accounts during episodes of inflation accelerates the decline in the demand for the domestic currency. Internal convertibility substitutes for the development of parallel black markets in foreign exchange, which governments are often unable to control in any case.

EXTERNAL FINANCING. Foreign direct investment by multinational companies can provide a quick means of integrating the domestic economy into the global trading system, as well as providing a source of capital and technology transfer. As discussed in a later section, such investment inflows have been very large in China, and foreign firms account for a large proportion of that country's exports. To date, the volume of investment in Central Europe and the former Soviet Union has been surprisingly low. The lack of capital inflows is due to problems within the domestic economy rather than problems of convertibility. Unlike China, the countries of Central Europe have been reluctant to grant concessions to foreign firms, and the internal reforms have not matured to the point that the countries are perceived as providing good investment opportunities. The economic and political environment in these countries is still considered too unstable for investment opportunities to be competitive with those in other regions of the global economy.

36. McKinnon (1991).

China has the advantage of a large number of Chinese overseas, particularly in Taiwan and Hong Kong, who are eager to serve as its agents in building links with the international economy. It is predominantly attractive as a source of inexpensive assembly-line labor. Its approach to developing a trade sector, however, is unlikely to be applicable to the other transitional economies.

Except in Hungary, foreign participation in the privatization process has also been extremely limited, in part because of government policies. At the same time, purchasing existing enterprises is not a particularly attractive option for foreign firms. They can earn a far better operating profit by starting new enterprises; moreover, the ownership rights to real estate and other assets of existing firms remain ambiguous.

Although the transitional economies have received external financial assistance, there is some question as to its precise extent.[37] Official agencies often report high levels of assistance to these economies. The IMF, for example, estimates that its external financing to the Central European countries amounted to about $40 billion in the 1991–93 period.[38] Such estimates, however, include substantial trade credits with very limited concessional finance and debt relief on old loans that could not have been repaid in any case. More traditional forms of foreign assistance, such as grants, have played a minor role in the transition process.

PAYMENTS UNIONS. With the collapse of CMEA trade in 1991 and the sharp decline in trade among the republics of the former Soviet Union, their governments began entertaining the idea of forming payments unions, similar to the one established in Western Europe after World War II, as a transitional arrangement.[39] A payments union eliminates the need to settle bilateral trade balances in a convertible currency. Instead, a member country can use its surplus with one member country to settle its deficit with another. Furthermore, individual countries can run a cumulative deficit with the union as a whole up to a certain quota, after which they must make payments in a convertible currency. Similarly, cumulative surplus countries can receive convertible currency payments up to a specified limit.

---

37. This issue is discussed more fully in subsequent sections on specific economies.
38. IMF (1994e).
39. Bofinger (1991).

Several objections were raised to such a union, however.[40] First, Russia was at the center of the former system in providing energy and raw materials in exchange for low-grade manufactured products. It was not interested in continuing the system of implicit subsidies when it could sell its natural resources in the global market. Second, the depth of the Soviet economic collapse implied a sharply reduced demand for the products of the other member countries. Third, the level of trade among the other CMEA countries was relatively low, and the continuation of trade on a nonconvertible basis was contrary to their strong preference for stronger economic ties with Western Europe.[41] Trade with the West was seen as an important route to modernization. Furthermore, politics played a large role. In the early 1990s the process of reform in the Soviet Union could not be viewed as irreversible, and the Central European states wanted to move quickly to establish their own independence and strengthen their identification with Western Europe.

Some analysts still think a payments union might be appropriate for the republics of the CIS since interrepublic trade could again be important in the future. But the interest is greater among outsiders than in the member republics, which are extremely distrustful of the Moscow government.[42] A payments union remains of limited value in the present circumstances because these economies are still on the brink of extreme macroeconomic instability. Nor can it operate if it is simply to be a mechanism through which Russia provides assistance to the other republics. What is more likely to emerge is an improved multilateral settlement system among these countries.

OVERVIEW. Within Central Europe, most countries have moved quickly to liberalize the trade regime. Poland and Czechoslovakia have established full current account convertibility and a unified single exchange rate and have converted the old system of quotas and import licenses to a relatively low and uniform level of tariffs. Hungary has followed much the same path. These three countries are also members of GATT and have signed association agreements with the

---

40. Kenen (1991); Rosati (1992).

41. Poland, Hungary, and the former Czechoslovakia did agree to form a free-trade zone, but it has little implication for trade flows.

42. Some republics have expressed an interest in greater cooperation as they rediscover the importance of their prior interdependence. Much of it is still based on the prospect of receiving energy at subsidized prices, however.

Table 1-2. *GDP per Capita in the Transitional Economies, 1992*

| | At purchasing power parity | | At the market exchange rate | |
| | U.S. dollars | Percent of U.S. | U.S. dollars | Percent of U.S. |
Economy				
Bulgaria	4,362	18.6	1,275	5.4
Czechoslovakia	5,844	24.9	2,397	10.2
Hungary	4,950	21.1	3,415	14.5
Poland	3,980	16.9	2,185	9.3
Romania	2,368	10.1	854	3.6
Russia	5,000	21.3	546	2.3
Ukraine	3,750	15.0	365	1.6
China	1,400	6.0	436	1.9
United States	23,500	. . .	. . .	. . .

Sources: Authors' calculations. PPP figures based on data from OECD (1993a). GDP at PPP for Central Europe is the OECD level for 1990 adjusted to 1992 using the percentage change in output over the intervening period. Russia and Ukraine are linked to Central Europe using the relative levels to Hungary published by the World Bank (1993e, p. 297). China's figure is estimated using several sources. Market exchange rate figures calculated from data found in World Bank (1994b). Exchange rate data are from IMF (1994d). Czechoslovakia's figures also based on OECD (1994b). Russia's exchange rate is from IMF (1993e). The same exchange rate is used for Ukraine because the World Bank calculation for GDP in 1992 is in rubles.

European Union that will result in expanded market access. Other transitional countries have also taken significant steps toward introducing convertible currencies, generally providing foreign exchange to importers, and eliminating the state monopoly on trade. All of these countries have also found it difficult to enforce controls on capital account transactions when other countries have open capital markets.

Initially, the pent-up demand for Western products, the desire to avoid holding financial assets in the domestic currency during the transition period, low levels of foreign exchange reserves, and difficulties in producing products suitable for Western markets all combined to exert downward pressure on the real exchange rates in these countries. Table 1-2 provides a comparison of estimates of GDP per capita based on purchasing power parity (PPP) and market exchange rates. According to PPP-based measures of income, GDP per capita in the stronger Central European economies is about 20–25 percent of U.S. levels. Yet income per capita (at 1992 market exchange rates) averaged about half the PPP values. The situation was far more extreme in the most unstable economies, such as Russia and Ukraine, where the market exchange rate implies that GDP per capita has declined to an absurd 2 percent of that of the United States.

A depreciated exchange rate can be beneficial in encouraging exports, but it does imply large losses in the terms of trade and thus a depressed domestic demand. Furthermore, it causes foreign capital measured in domestic wage units to shoot up in price and thus pushes these economies toward labor-intensive production processes that may be inappropriate in the post-transition era. It also means that foreign competition cannot restrain domestic prices, nor provide an effective guide for the domestic price structure.

An extreme example is provided by the situation in Russia. With the collapse of the ruble, domestic prices for goods traded in world markets would have skyrocketed in the absence of controls. If its energy output, a highly marketable product, were priced at world levels in 1992, domestic energy consumption would have exceeded the nation's GDP by a factor of two.[43] As a result, the government felt compelled to use a substantial portion of its export earnings to subsidize the costs of critical imported materials used in domestic production and to maintain price controls for basic consumption items.

The Sequence of Reform—Revolution versus Evolution

Perhaps the most intense debate over economic reform has occurred between those calling for a revolutionary and rapid pace of reform, "shock therapy," and those promoting a more evolutionary or gradual pace of change.[44] The advocates of rapid reform believe that both economic and political problems need to be addressed immediately, through a dismantling of the old institutions of state control. Conceptually, they draw their view of economic agents from the informed-rational-actor model, in which the critical action is to confront economic agents with the incentives of a laissez-faire economy, private property rights, and monetary stability as soon as possible: in other words, get the incentives right, and everything else will take care

43. Authors' calculations. Of course, if energy prices were at world levels, the output of the energy sector and thus GDP would have been valued far higher, but the required redistribution of incomes would still be incredible.

44. Many writers have contributed to this debate. Brada (1993) and Murrell (1993) provide contrasting views and extensive references.

of itself. On the political front, change must occur quickly before its opponents can become organized; furthermore, the change must be extensive enough to ensure that there is no going back. Dismantling the old system is as great a priority as building something new. In this view, the benefits of moving from a centrally planned to a market economy are said to be large, compared with the small and uncertain benefits of gradual change.

The evolutionists, in contrast, stress the role of past experience in shaping the behavior of economic agents who do not have perfect knowledge. They also believe that if change is too rapid it can lead to collapse rather than adjustment: institutions cannot simply be imported but must be created from within in order to have legitimacy. The evolutionists accuse the shock therapists of adopting the techniques of the Marxists they seek to replace, since they would impose radical reforms from above rather than allow them to evolve from below. The evolutionists also believe that there are substantial benefits to implementing reforms in the correct sequence, and that any reform program must be tailored to the specific situation of each country. From the political perspective, gradualists argue for an initial emphasis on reforms that yield relatively quick benefits in order to build majority support for what must be seen as a process stretching over many years. They argue that the initial large losses of a shock program would generate a political and social backlash that would derail the reform process.

This controversy erupted after Poland introduced a severe macroeconomic stabilization program, combined with domestic price liberalization and current account convertibility, at the beginning of 1990. The resulting collapse of real output led critics to argue that the government had overreacted and introduced measures that were too extreme. Yet the striking feature of the decline in output was that it occurred throughout the transitional economies of Central Europe, regardless of whether they undertook rapid reform, gradual reform, or did nothing. Poland was an example of a "big bang" only in the stabilization sphere, where it faced the unique problem of hyperinflation and had little choice but to address the issue quickly.[45] It did move rapidly to liberalize prices and establish current account con-

---

45. There is considerable evidence from the experience of other high-inflation countries that a shock program is most effective in dealing with situations of high inflation. Far less is known about the choice between a rapid and a gradual introduction of microeconomic reforms. See Bruno (1992).

vertibility; but in other areas of reform, Poland has gone forward at about the same pace as the other Central European countries. The shock therapy program has been stopped, but few of its initial actions have been reversed. The controversy has reemerged, however, in the light of events in Russia.

The other country of substantial interest in regard to the pace of reform is China. It began the process of economic reform far earlier than the others, and at a time when it still had some central control at the political level. From the beginning, the Chinese viewed the reform process as one of evolutionary change: their goal was to gradually decentralize the economy, while trying to maintain some central control over the political system.[46] In contrast, Central Europe has approached economic reform as a process of revolutionary change, attempting to compress the process of shifting over to a market economy into a very short time period and arguing that the sequence of the reforms matters little if one does everything at once.

The Chinese strategy differs most notably from that of Eastern Europe in the areas of price liberalization, privatization, financial measures, and trade policy.[47] China acted quickly to liberalize prices in agriculture and small enterprises but maintained control over the prices of the large enterprises. The reform process also began in the absence of severe repressed inflation. Thus China could allow state orders to claim part of an enterprise's output and yet permit producers to sell any surplus in a parallel free market. The prices were different, but in most years the amount was not significant enough to affect the state orders. Over time, the proportion of output subject to state orders declined. Furthermore, the state enterprises were not allowed to compete against each other for supplies. Nor were they allowed to bid for foreign exchange. These restrictions were important because a system of free prices cannot be expected to operate if buyers do not have hard budget constraints. State enterprises were encouraged to compete against one another, however, in the sale of their output.

---

46. This point can be overemphasized because the actual changes often emerged out of compromises between opposing groups, rather than as a planned strategy. For a detailed report on the Chinese reform process with some lessons for Eastern Europe see Gelb, Jefferson, and Singh (1993).

47. This contrast is highlighted in a paper by McKinnon (1993b), from which the following discussion is drawn.

Second, China opened to the global market on a gradual basis, by first establishing special enterprise zones in which exporters could deal freely in a convertible currency with foreign firms. The distinction between the special economic zones and the rest of the economy was allowed to erode over time.

Third, China dealt with the weakness of the financial system by denying the new nonstate sector extensive access to bank credit—the idea was to force it to self-finance its expansion—and by continuing to closely regulate the access of the state enterprises to credit. At the same time, interest rates on deposits were generally positive in real terms so as to maintain saving incentives. In effect, bank deposits were reserved to finance the government budget and the deficits of state-owned enterprises. Like the other countries in transition, China did not act quickly to introduce an efficient tax system and suffered from an erosion of public revenues, but a high level of private saving ensured that the budget deficits could be financed without adding greatly to inflation pressures.

The Chinese approach reflected an acute awareness of the special problems created by the state enterprises, which could not be expected to operate effectively in a free market in which they were not subject to hard budget constraints.[48] It is also distinguishable from the approach in Central Europe in that it emphasized new enterprises, rather than attempting to reform the old ones. The political and economic differences between China and Central Europe, not to mention Russia, are substantial enough, however, to warn against any simple conclusions about the relative effectiveness of different approaches to reform.[49] In China, for example, the reform measures have drawn workers away from agriculture to industry, a process in which everyone has been made better off. In contrast significant portions of the population in Central Europe and Russia fear that the reallocation among industrial workers will bring economic loss.

The situation in Russia is even more complex, for although the economy has collapsed, it is not clear that reform alone is to blame. The central government lost control and never had the legitimacy of governments in Central Europe. The breakup of the former Soviet Union, on top of the collapse of the CMEA, was a great shock to the

48. The argument against the Chinese approach of parallel markets for the state enterprises is laid out in Murphy, Shleifer, and Vishny (1992).

49. Woo (1993); Sachs and Woo (1993).

economy, but it may not have been avoided simply by proceeding at a slower pace. Within the former Soviet republics and Russia itself there is enormous distrust and contempt for any government that makes it difficult to have a "planned reform" process controlled from above. The center is trying to force and direct the process of economic transition, while everything else, from political administration to the collection of taxes, is becoming more decentralized. For a time, even the monetary system operated with competing central banks disbursing the ruble. The government designed a "shock therapy" program along the lines of Poland's program in 1992 but never had the ability to implement it fully.

Many of the issues that divide the shock therapists and the gradualists have become moot because the major elements of reform have been put in place in many countries, or because governments have lost the authority to control the reform program, as is the case in several republics of the former Soviet Union. The most relevant aspect of the dispute at present concerns the approach to privatization. One side argues for a mass privatization of existing enterprises, ending what is perceived as a favored relationship with the government. The other side would concentrate scarce capital on developing new firms in the private sector, while maintaining direct controls on the state enterprises. In many countries, however, strong state control is no longer an option. The state-owned enterprises are in limbo, and the search is on for a second-best policy that would maximize the hard budget constraints. Privatization is consistent with the long-run objective, and there is no obviously superior short-run policy. Perhaps the only way to curtail the present practice of borrowing to cover losses would be to break up the state enterprises into smaller, less powerful units and reform the financial sector.

Chapter 2

China

SINCE 1978, China's GDP has grown at an average rate of 8.8 percent per year, in comparison with 3.0 percent in 1960–78. This is an enormous accomplishment for a country of more than a billion people.[1] That improved performance is the result of economic reform and the shift away from central planning to a market-oriented economy. As already mentioned, China's strategy of gradual and incremental reform contrasts sharply with the radical approach being taken in Central Europe and Russia. Furthermore, its central concern has been to develop markets, not private ownership. In fact, some have alleged that China's success was based on its ability to keep Western economic advisers at bay. Although China listened to outsiders, it tailored the reform to its own particular economic and political circumstances.

Shock therapy was rejected in China because the government feared that it would be too destabilizing, both politically and economically.[2] Sudden change would mean large-scale unemployment, civil unrest, and disruptive internal migration. At the same time, China did not work from a specific broad plan or strategy or even a clear idea of what the end result should be. In many cases, its gradualist approach

---

1. In making comparisons between China and other reforming economies, it is important to remember that they are at much different stages of development. Even after a decade of very rapid growth, GDP per capita in China was only about $1,200–$1,500 in 1992, as based on purchasing power parity. Gulde and Schulze-Ghattas (1993).

2. Shock therapy in the macroeconomic context was also unnecessary because China began its reforms with relative stability. Unlike Poland, for example, it did not face fiscal imbalances and rampant inflation at the outset.

39

was the result of compromise among strong competing political groups. Yet that gradualism has not necessarily been the key to China's success. Its greatest progress has been achieved in those sectors and provinces that embarked on rapid and far-reaching reform. Above all, reform has been pragmatic, focusing on what works.

Equally important, China has not directed its reforms from the center. What it has most clearly rejected is the strong hierarchical structure of central planning that dominated Central Europe and the former Soviet Union, replacing it with a system of substantial local administrative autonomy and a reliance on markets. Most of the important changes have been initiated at the local level in a pronounced pattern of trial and error, later followed by government ratification. The crucial early reforms were the liberalization of the rural economy, the partial liberalization of prices, and the opening to the global market.

Before 1978, the forced industrialization of the Chinese economy had been based on a sharp distinction between rural and urban areas. The price system was used to tax rural areas, which were inhabited by about 80 percent of the population, to finance industrialization in the urban areas. Goods delivered from rural areas—food, fuel, and raw materials—were valued at low state-set prices, while the flow back in the form of consumer goods was sold at high prices. In effect, standards of living in the urban areas were subsidized by the rural poor.

A brief overview of economic trends since 1980 (table 2-1) indicates that economic growth over the past fifteen years has consistently been close to 10 percent per year.[3] Inflation has been highly volatile, but has averaged much less than in the other transitional economies. Foreign trade has tripled as a share of GDP in this period, and China has attracted large volumes of foreign direct investment to augment a surprisingly high level of domestic saving. The growth of both trade and foreign investment is a simple measure of the new emphasis on opening China and increasing its interactions with the global economy. That fact that China is also becoming a more industrialized urban society is responsible for some of the increased social and political tensions.

---

3. As explained later, the phenomenal growth of the Chinese economy is not reflected in dollar measures of GDP because of a steadily depreciating real exchange rate.

Table 2-1. *Selected Economic Indicators, China, 1980–92*

Indicator	1980–85	1985–90	1990–92
Average real GDP growth (percent)	10.0	7.3	11.1
Average real GDP per capita growth (percent)	8.5	5.6	9.2
Average inflation rate (percent)	4.2	10.6	5.1
Average overall budgetary balance/GDP (percent)	–1.8	–1.9	–2.8

	1980	1985	1990	1992
Nominal GDP (billions of U.S. dollars)	298	291	370	432
Nominal GDP per capita (U.S. dollars)	304	277	326	372
Population (millions)	981	1,051	1,134	1,162
Exports/GDP (percent)	6.1	9.4	16.8	19.8
Imports/GDP (percent)	6.7	14.5	14.4	18.8
GDP at factor cost (percent)	100	100	100	. . .
Agriculture	34	31	27	. . .
Industry	38	39	48	. . .
Services	28	30	25	. . .
Urban population (percent of labor force)	19	37	56	. . .
Foreign direct investment (billions of U.S. dollars)	0.4	2.0	3.8	11.3
Total external debt/GDP (percent)	1.5	5.7	14.2	16.0

Sources: World Bank (1994b, pp. 184–85); International Monetary Fund (1993d, pp. 278–81); World Bank (1993d, p. 90); Bell, Khor, and Kochhar (1993, p. 62).

Rural Reform

The Chinese reforms began in agriculture. The first step was to raise prices and replace the commune system of production teams and assigned quotas with individual family farms. In the early 1980s the government introduced a system of contracts that required individual households to supply their share of the production team's quota. Households were then free to dispose of any surplus as they saw fit. Land was not privatized, but it was assigned to individual households for periods of five years, later extended to fifteen. Furthermore, the government substantially increased the price that it paid farmers for the quota output; farmers soon gained another source of income from the free markets that grew up around agricultural output in excess of contract levels. The result was a large surge in agricultural output, which grew at twice the rate of the preceding two decades. Gains in productivity also created substantial surplus labor, which was in turn absorbed by the development of township and village enterprises that produce industrial products.

The township and village enterprises are formally collectively owned. The innovation introduced was that they were allowed to sell their output at market prices, retain the profits, and reinvest their earnings. These enterprises were promoted by local governments because they were a source of revenue and jobs; in addition, they were immediately subject to hard budget constraints because the lower administrative units of government had limited access to cheap credit. Another distinctive feature of the local enterprises is that they do not report to any industrial ministry. As of 1992 they employed about 100 million of China's rural work force of 430 million and accounted for about one-fourth of total industrial output. An additional 30 million individuals are employed in small private businesses.[4] In contrast, the work force of the urban state-owned enterprises and collectives has remained at the same level since the early 1980s. About half of township and village output is in light manufactures, but a surprising number of these local enterprises are in direct competition with the SOEs in heavy industry. They are also active in the export sector.[5] One of the most interesting aspects of the rural reform is that it has side-stepped the issue of privatization, emphasizing instead the conversion to markets and incentives for effective control and management of the enterprises.

Urban Reform

The liberalization of the rural sector has had its costs: the relative standards of income in the cities have declined, and political unrest among what had been the privileged has increased. The government did not immediately pass the full cost of higher farm prices on to the retail level. Instead it relied on large subsidies that strained the budget. Over time, rural price reform imposed losses on the relative

4. Bell, Khor, and Kochhar (1993, pp. 16–17).
5. World Bank (1994a, p. 14).

income position of city dwellers. The gradual reduction in their subsidies highlighted their low productivity and contributed to the student and worker demonstrations of the late 1980s. The response of the government after 1984 was to shift its attention to reforming the state-owned enterprises and to expand markets into the urban sector in an effort to generate the same efficiency gains that accompanied the rural reforms.

The pattern established in agriculture—incremental change with a large concern for the sequence of reform—was then adopted in the urban sector. The objective there was to liberalize prices and rely on markets further. For price reform to work, however, the management of enterprises must be able to respond to changing market signals, varying its labor force to changing opportunities. Thus the government decided to follow the sequence of labor market reform, management reform, and then price liberalization.

Sequencing can only be a matter of degree, however. China cannot delay price liberalization to the end of a process of reforming the state enterprises. Managements cannot make rational decentralized decisions under a severely distorted price system. Thus price liberalization is a continuous process that occurs in step with reforms in labor markets and management practices. Interestingly, the question of privatization almost never arises.

By relying on the enterprises to provide a broad range of social services—including housing, medical care, and education—the government is severely limited in its ability to subject these enterprises to hard budget constraints without unacceptable unemployment consequences. This approach is beginning to change: a substantial number of firms were declared bankrupt in 1992, which signaled the beginning of a policy of applying the bankruptcy laws. Unemployment is also becoming a significant issue. And although the government continues to own the state enterprises, management control is shifting to the enterprises.

During the 1980s the state enterprises were granted increased autonomy and allowed to retain some of their profits, make decisions on most investment, and participate in a contracting system that allowed any surplus to be sold in the free market. However, prices on state deliveries continued to be controlled, tax rates and access to subsidized credit and raw materials were subject to negotiation, and loss-making firms were subsidized. Only recently has management been allowed to dismiss redundant labor in some cases. New workers are hired on a contract basis rather than as life-time employees. Evidence on the success of these reforms is decidedly mixed, and the enterprises continue to absorb a large portion of credit to cover their losses.[6] However, an estimated 70 percent of the losses recorded by state-owned enterprises result from government price controls in areas such as energy and transportation.[7] Because of these controls, energy and raw material industries register losses, while processing industries appear more profitable than they truly are.

The extent to which the industrial reforms have improved the efficiency of the state enterprises is still uncertain. Thus far, the most effective policy has been to let them decline in relative importance: their share of industrial output fell from 76 percent in 1982 to 46 percent in 1991, and this figure is expected to decline to about 25 percent by 1999. Meanwhile, the share of output supplied by rural industries has increased from 10 to 33 percent. Note, however, that the output of the state enterprises grew at an annual rate of 7.8 percent over the 1980–91 period, so it would be inaccurate to say that they stagnated.[8]

It is extremely difficult to evaluate the performance of the state enterprises because the prices of both their inputs and output are still subject to substantial government control. Furthermore, they are responsible for a vast array of social programs, the cost of which is commingled with the production accounts, and they still contribute a disproportionate share of government revenue. A study by Woo and others using data from a sample of state enterprises for the 1984–88 period concludes that the growth in labor productivity within these enterprises was attributable to the extensive use of capital, with little evidence of gain in total factor productivity.[9] In contrast, McGuckin and Nguyen find sharp improvements in productivity growth after 1984, but larger gains in the collective and private firms than in the state enterprises.[10] Three other studies also conclude that some improvement is taking place.[11] A convergence of profit rates across

6. Woo and others (1993).

7. Bell, Khor, and Kochhar (1993, p. 29).

8. Sachs and Woo (1993, table 6).

9. Woo and others (1993).

10. McGuckin and Nguyen (1993).

11. Jefferson, Rawski, and Zheng (1992); McMillan and Naughton (1992); and Rawski (1994).

industries suggests that the state enterprises are losing some of their monopoly power.[12] The general view is that about one-third of these enterprises could be successful in a completely open market, whereas the others would require extensive restructuring or have to be closed. There is no question that the state-owned enterprises have performed less well than the collectives and private firms, and that they continue to absorb and waste a disproportionate share of national saving.

Despite its successes, China is far from having completed the transition to a market economy. In 1992 about 80 percent of retail trade was based on free-market prices, but at earlier stages of processing about one-third of agricultural and industrial output remained subject to state control or guidance.[13] The dual price system, under which above-plan output could be sold in the market, has worked less well in the industrial sector than in agriculture. It has led to substantial corruption and encouraged firms to negotiate high levels of subsidized inputs and low quotas for plan output, leaving them free to sell in the more lucrative free market. The system is being phased out in favor of uniform market prices, and the vast proportion of transactions should be at free market prices within the next few years. The mobility of labor remains low, because the supply of housing is still closely tied to the enterprises; and rents, although they are being progressively increased, also remain very low. Furthermore, individuals cannot move internally without the permission of the authorities. Although energy prices have been increased, they continue to be heavily subsidized.

Progress has also been surprisingly slow in the reform of China's fiscal and financial systems. As shown in table 2-2, the budget has suffered from the same erosion of revenues that accompanied reform in the other centrally planned economies. Profit remittances of the state enterprises, which previously accounted for the bulk of government revenue, have declined sharply in recent years. Total revenues have dropped from 29.4 percent of GDP in 1980 to 16.6 percent in 1992. China has begun relying more on taxes, including a VAT, but tax revenues have also fallen sharply since the mid-1980s. The system of sharing revenue between the central and local governments has worked poorly and has been a continuing source of tension. Taxes on

12. Naughton (1992).
13. Bell, Khor, and Kochhar (1993, p. 27).

Table 2-2. *Developments in China's Budget, 1980–92*
Percent of GDP

Item	1980	1985	1990	1992
Total revenue	29.4	26.7	19.9	16.6
Tax revenue	12.8	25.6	17.7	14.2
Taxes on income and profits	1.7	8.6	4.8	3.2
Taxes on goods and services	10.4	11.3	8.7	8.7
Product tax	0.0	6.9	3.3	2.9
VAT	0.0	1.7	2.3	3.0
Business tax	0.0	2.5	2.9	2.8
Real estate tax	0.0	0.0	0.2	0.0
Taxes of international trade	0.8	2.4	0.9	0.9
Other taxes	0.0	3.3	3.3	1.5
Nontax revenues	16.6	1.1	2.1	2.4
Total expenditure and net lending	32.8	27.2	22.0	19.1
Current expenditure	22.2	19.6	17.3	15.2
Administrative	1.5	1.7	1.9	1.8
Defense	4.4	2.2	1.6	1.6
Culture, education, public health	3.5	3.7	3.5	3.3
Economic services	4.3	2.6	2.1	2.0
Social welfare relief	0.0	0.0	0.3	0.3
Subsidies	6.1	5.9	5.4	3.2
Daily necessities	5.4	3.7	2.2	1.3
Enterprise losses	0.8	2.1	3.3	1.9
Other	2.4	3.5	2.5	3.0
Development expenditure	10.6	7.5	4.6	3.9
Budget balance	−3.4	−0.5	−2.1	2.5

Source: World Bank (1992, table 7.5)

personal income and land are still virtually nonexistent. On the expenditure side, in addition to the decline in public capital investment, there has been little effort to develop a social safety net or to move the provision of social services outside of the enterprises. In 1992, subsidies still accounted for 17 percent of government outlays.[14] The result has been consistent budget deficits that are financed though credits from the state banks.

14. A portion of the subsidies could be viewed as a substitute for an effective set of public social programs; and their elimination does not imply an equal net gain to the budget. Some of them resemble large unemployment insurance programs, but with weak incentives to find alternative employment.

In the financial area, China converted to a two-tier banking system in the early 1980s. That action had the unintended result of weakening the government's control over the relationship between the banks and the enterprises, further softening the budget constraint on their operations. In recent years, domestic bank financing of state enterprises has represented about 10 percent of GDP. Lending is still strongly influenced by political factors, particularly at the local level. The proportions of bad loans at the state banks are comparable to those observed in Central Europe. Thus the central bank is faced with the choice of continuing to finance local lending or precipitating a financial crisis.[15]

Like other transitional economies, China has been financing substantial budget deficits and loans to loss-making state enterprises through the financial system. The difference is that this financing has not resulted in high and destabilizing rates of inflation. In contrast to the other economies, China benefits from high levels of private saving and the willingness of households to deposit their savings in the state banks. Real rates of return on those deposits have generally been positive. Thus China is usually able to finance the budget deficits and enterprise losses out of household bank deposits, rather than excessive money creation.[16] Household term deposits at banks, for example, grew at three times the rate of GDP between 1984 and 1992, rising from 13 percent of GDP to 39 percent. The high rate of private saving provides China with a margin of safety not available to the other transitional economies. It can use capital inefficiently and still maintain strong growth. Growth has been surprisingly extensive, particularly within the state enterprises. The increases in capital per worker, rather than gains in total factor productivity, have been responsible for a high share of the gain in output per worker. The share of GDP devoted to fixed capital formation averaged 30 percent over the 1985–92 period.[17]

China's macroeconomic stabilization policies have been adversely affected, however, by the lack of a strong fiscal system and its slow

15. At the end of 1992, 27 percent of the liabilities of the state specialized and universal banks consisted of loans from the central bank. In contrast, 98 percent of the liabilities of rural credit cooperatives consisted of deposits, and 82 percent of those deposits were owned by individuals (World Bank, 1992, tables 6.4 and 6.5).

16. McKinnon (1993a).

17. World Bank (1992, table 4).

approach to financial reform. The economy has been plagued by several episodes of excessive inflation that disrupted the growth process. With the financial reforms still incomplete, the central bank must depend on a mixture of direct (administrative) and indirect (interest rates) controls on credit creation. The provincial authorities and enterprises have become increasingly adept at circumventing the administrative controls though nonstate sources of credit, and the state enterprises that are not subject to hard budget constraints are insensitive to variations in interest costs. The loss-making enterprises continue to seek credit regardless of the interest rate, and their loan requests are supported by local political administrators. The provincial banks get around the monetary policy by continuing to support the local state enterprises on the assumption that they will be bailed out by the central bank. If the central bank attempts to impose constraints on loans, they will fall heavily on the most dynamic sector of the economy: the township and village enterprises and private firms. At the same time, the lack of a strong tax base and continued reliance on revenues of the state enterprises make it difficult to use fiscal policy as an effective tool of macroeconomic control.

Because of its deteriorating revenue situation and continued reliance on large subsidies, the government has greatly underinvested in the social infrastructure. As a result, the country's transportation system is inadequate, which in turn has made it difficult to integrate the domestic economy, achieve efficiency gains, and encourage the inland provinces to participate in the growth of trade and national output. As a share of GDP, capital expenditures within the national budget have declined to one-third of their 1978 level, largely at the expense of transportation. Adjusted for population and the amount of arable land, China's rail system and highway systems are the smallest of any major economy.[18] Its rail system is one-sixth that of the United States and half that of the former Soviet Union. Its road network is less than a tenth of that of the United States and far below that of other economies at similar levels of development.

Transportation is to receive a higher priority in the 1990s, with the main financing to be generated internally. The government has substantially reduced its taxation of the industry and has obtained some international funds. Highway financing is to be provided through an

18. World Bank (1992).

expanded system of user fees. Yet China still makes no use of taxes on motor fuels as a source of revenue. There is also no significant independent, or common-carrier, trucking industry.

Foreign Sector Liberalization

The third large area of reform was the external sector. China has experienced an enormous expansion of its trade since beginning its reforms in 1978, but the actual liberalization of trade did not really get under way until the mid-1980s. Up to 1984, trade remained by and large under the control of the state, and its composition suggested that its primary objective was just to finance necessary imports, rather than to exploit any comparative advantage. Exports consisted mainly of petroleum and primary commodities. After 1985, the composition of exports began to shift strongly toward labor-intensive light manufactures, such as apparel and electronic components.[19]

The growth of trade and the change in its composition so as to exploit areas of comparative advantage can be traced to several measures: decentralization permitted the growth of a large number of foreign trade corporations; reforms in the pricing of traded goods brought the domestic prices of both exports and imports in line with those of world markets; and the aggressive use of exchange rate devaluations promoted exports.[20] But the gradual nature of those reforms and the extent to which the government controlled the process also had some effect.

Before the 1980s, the domestic price of traded goods was cut off from global markets. The price of imports was set on the basis of the price of comparable domestically produced goods, not their cost in world markets. Similarly, the trading corporations purchased goods for export as specified under the central plan, and at domestic prices, and they rebated all subsequent foreign exchange earnings to the government.

The reforms changed that system. By the mid-1980s, the domestic price of four-fifths of all imports was based on their import cost, and

19. World Bank (1994a, pp. 6–10).

20. These reforms and their consequences are detailed in Lardy (1992), which is the basis for the following summary.

that ratio rose to more than 90 percent by the early 1990s.[21] On the export side, firms were free to seek the most favorable price from competing trading companies for more than half of exports, and state enterprises were free to sell output in excess of state orders in the international market.

In the early 1980s the twelve state-owned foreign trade corporations lost their monopoly power, and by the late 1980s there were more than 5,000 general trading companies. But the government licensed such firms, and at the end of the decade it acted to close or merge those whose performance had been unsatisfactory, leaving about 4,000 firms in the early 1990s.[22] By 1993 only about 15 percent of exports and 20 percent of imports remained subject to the government's plan. To attract foreign direct investment, China introduced special economic zones in the coastal areas and gave them preferential tax and tariff treatment.

With the change in the domestic pricing of tradable goods, variations in the exchange rate began to have an impact on domestic production decisions. Starting from an overvalued position in the early 1980s, the real exchange rate was allowed to depreciate, on a trade-weighted basis, by about 60 percent over the last half of the 1980s.[23] The government also altered its exchange regulations to allow firms to retain a portion of their foreign exchange earnings. However, it maintained a high level of tariffs that continued to favor the domestic production of consumer goods.

The Trade Regime

Despite the liberalization that has occurred, China's current trading system is complex and strongly distorted by government policies. Direct administrative controls over exports and imports have been reduced, but the average tariff rate, about 32 percent on a trade-weighted basis, is high by international standards. The tariffs among commodity groups also vary greatly. At the same time, the effective tariff, measured by tariff revenues as a percentage of imports, amounts to 6 percent of import value, which is among the lowest

21. Lardy (1992, p. 704).
22. Bell, Khor, and Kochhar (1993, p. 75).
23. Lardy (1992, p. 707).

effective tariffs of the developing economies.[24] The explanation for this dichotomy lies in the numerous government grants of exemptions and rebates, and what appears to be significant tariff evasion. The combination of high tariffs and low collections implies a highly distortionary tariff structure.

In addition, China relies on an intricate system of nontariff barriers that affect about 50 percent of total imports. Roughly 20 percent of total imports are still subject to the import plan, normally because their domestic prices are substantially out of line with world prices. Import licensing is required for an additional 12 percent, quantitative import controls cover about 8 percent, and 14 percent are restricted to specific foreign trade corporations.[25] Thus administrative controls, with their potential for discriminatory treatment, are still a prominent feature of the import regime.

On the export side, the role of formal planning has declined to about 15 percent of the total, but export licensing is applied to another 15 percent.[26] These controls are used primarily to maintain the domestic price of a few selected products below world levels, and to appropriate the rents that would otherwise be earned on products that are not completely free of domestic controls.

China relies heavily on foreign trading companies to act as intermediaries between domestic firms and the foreign market. Such trading companies play only a small role in the United States and Europe, but they have been an important historical feature of several Asian economies, particularly Japan. These companies serve as the distributional network for domestic producers, often provide working capital, and procure required supplies and equipment. They also act as conduits for information on technology, product design, and packaging appropriate for the foreign market. On the export side, the Chinese foreign trading companies generally take title to the products and absorb all the risks of marketing. On the import side, they more often act as simple agents in obtaining goods for domestic clients. They process about 90 percent of China's exports and 80 percent of its imports.[27] These companies are linked to trading firms in Hong

24. World Bank (1994a, p. 56).
25. World Bank (1994a, pp. 63–67). China has announced plans to reduce further the role of the nontariff barriers.
26. World Bank (1994a, pp. 67–68).
27. World Bank (1994a, p. 113).

Kong, and about 50 percent of China's exports pass through Hong Kong.[28]

China is not yet a member of GATT. In 1986 it requested that the membership it terminated in 1950 be resumed. However, other countries argue that continuing administrative controls on some portions of trade violates the basic provision of GATT, which specifies that countries should rely on tariffs and exchange rates as the primary means of regulating trade. This issue is discussed more fully in a later section.

On the other side of the market, China's trade is heavily affected by the quantitative restrictions of importing countries. About half of all trade with the United States is in categories covered by various nontariff barriers; this figure is 30 percent for the trade with Europe and 22 percent for the trade with Japan.[29] These proportions are considerably greater than those for other developing countries and are largely the result of the product composition of China's exports, which are dominated by clothing and textiles.[30] A recent study by the World Bank estimated that a 50 percent reduction in the trade protection of the United States, Japan, and the European Union would increase Chinese exports by 30–40 percent.[31] Although most countries grant MFN status to Chinese exports, China is not eligible for the generalized system of preferences (GSP) accorded to other developing countries.

Special Economic Zones

The special economic zones have greatly contributed to the rapid growth of China's exports and helped it attract foreign investments. Three such zones were established in Guangdong Province and one in Fujian in 1979–80. The local authorities within these zones have considerably greater administrative autonomy than those elsewhere in the country, and they can provide far more generous incentives to both domestic producers and foreign firms. They can undertake their own investment projects outside the central plan, enterprises in the zones enjoy much lower rates of taxation than those outside them,

28. World Bank (1994a, p. 13).

29. World Bank (1994a, p. 148).

30. The proportion of trade covered by nontariff barriers can also be misleading because it does not reflect the level of imports at which the barriers are binding. Imports of clothing into the United States, for example, are far higher than for Europe and Japan, even though the latter applies no formal restrictions.

31. World Bank (1994a, p. 151).

and the enterprises are free to make their own production and marketing decisions. All imports for production that are reexported or used within the zone are duty free.

China treated the zones as laboratories in which it could experiment with a faster pace of economic liberalization than in the country as a whole. Without doubt, they have achieved impressive economic gains. With only 0.2 percent of the population, in 1991 they accounted for about 14 percent of China's exports, 16 percent of foreign direct investment, and a level of GDP per capita six times that of China as a whole.[32] Their apparent success has led to the creation of a fifth special enterprise zone and fourteen open coastal cities.

The enormous size of the incentives accorded to enterprises (both domestic and foreign) within the zones suggests, however, that much of the gain may have occurred at the expense of other regions of China. The incentives effectively raised the cost of investing in the other regions, and as halfway houses between the socialist system of China and the external economy, the zones have had enormous opportunities to profit from pure rent-seeking. Furthermore, it would appear from the trade data that some of the export growth of the special zones represented a simple displacement of low-level processing operations from Hong Kong and Taiwan to the mainland, particularly in apparel. The more lasting value of the zones lies in the lessons they provided and the fact that they encouraged the authorities to expand the liberalization programs to China as a whole. For example, the duty-free import of material and supplies for reexport was extended on a national basis in 1984. Such processing-based exports have grown to account for 64 percent of China's manufactured exports, while the share of the zones is declining.[33] Incentives for foreign investment that were originally restricted to these zones have been broadened to the national level.

Foreign Exchange Regime

Until very recently, China has maintained a convoluted dual exchange rate regime. In the last half of the 1980s, exporters surren-

32. Bell, Khor, and Kochhar (1993, p. 34). The export share of 14 percent may be overstated if the special enterprise zones serve as export centers for the surrounding area. A more conservative estimate would be about 10 percent of the total.

33. World Bank (1994a, p. 11).

dered their foreign exchange to the government and were issued retention quotas for a share of those earnings. These quotas could be bought and sold in foreign exchange adjustment centers. Since 1988 the "swap market" has operated as an auction market, and the rate has consistently been below (depreciated) the official rate. The retention quotas varied substantially by industry and region, with a typical retention rate of 25 percent split equally between the foreign trading company and the producing enterprise. In 1991 the standard retention rate was raised to 80 percent, with 10 percent to the local government, 10 percent to the producing firm, and 60 percent to the trading company. In addition, the government had the right to buy another 30 percent at the swap market rate. It appears that the state has generally exercised that right, with the result that only about 50 percent of export earnings are available to finance nonplan imports.[34] Buyers' access to the adjustment centers was controlled by the government, but the precise rules varied by region and no attempt was made to integrate the centers on a national scale.

With the expansion of the swap market, market forces gradually came to play a role in the determination of the exchange rate. The effective exchange rate for exporters was a weighted average of the official and swap rates, the weights depending on the retention rate. The swap rate was the main determinant for nonplan imports. Before 1991 the official Chinese exchange rate was fixed to the dollar, with periodic nominal devaluations. Since early 1991 it has relied on a managed float with small adjustments at frequent intervals.

One surprising feature of the Chinese exchange rate has been the magnitude of the devaluation of the real rate over the reform period. As shown in figure 2-1, the dollar exchange rate has fallen to about one-fourth of its 1980 value. A trade-weighted index of the swap market rate, shown in figure 2-2, suggests that much of the effective devaluation took place before the opening of the swap market in 1988: the real swap rate has been fairly stable over the past five years.[35] However, the relative importance of the swap market rate has expanded over time because the retention rate has risen to 80 percent.

34. World Bank (1994a, pp. 30–31).
35. Enterprises were allowed to trade their retention quotas for domestic currency after 1980 but at officially set prices. In 1988 the government allowed the rate to be determined in the market, and the volume of transactions grew from about $6 billion in 1988 to $25 billion in 1992 (Khor, 1993).

Figure 2-1. *China's Exchange Rate, 1980–92*

Yuan per U.S. dollar

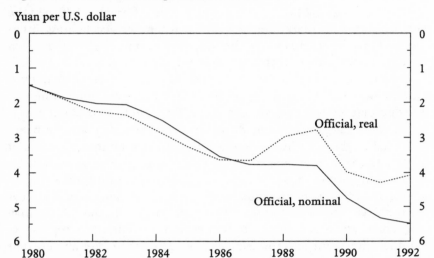

Source: Khor (1993). Values before 1987 based on authors' estimates.

Figure 2-2. *Official and Swap Market Exchange Rates, 1987–93*

Trade-weighted indexes of real values,   1980 = 100

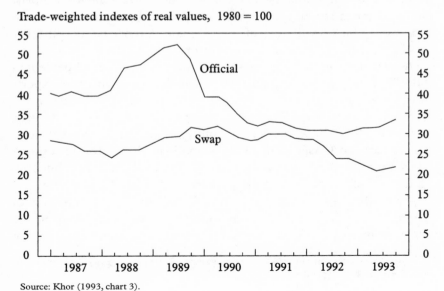

Source: Khor (1993, chart 3).

Thus the effective exchange rate has moved closer to the swap rate in the 1990s, implying further devaluation. The differential between the official and swap market rates widened whenever accelerating inflation led to an overvaluation of the official rate and at those times, such as 1992, when the government increased access to the swap market.

At the beginning of 1994, the exchange rate was unified by a devaluation of the official rate to the level of the swap market rate and the elimination of the retention system. The effective devaluation was relatively small, since about 80 percent of trade was already being financed at the swap rate. The government still limits the access of buyers to the market for foreign exchange, but the reform included a move to a national foreign exchange market operating through the banks and introduced the requirement that all foreign exchange must be purchased through the market. In the short run, the reform may tighten access to foreign exchange, but over the long run it represents another important step toward a unified national market and current account convertibility, in line with GATT requirements.

Results

The net result of China's reforms was to reverse the previous bias against external trade. Between 1980 and 1992 China's exports, adjusted for inflation, grew at an annual rate of 12.3 percent, which was twice the growth rate of global trade. China has become the world's tenth largest trader, moving up from thirtieth place in the mid-1970s. Total trade (exports plus imports) rose from 13 percent of GDP in 1980 to 38 percent in 1992.[36] Clearly, the expansion of exports was a leading factor behind China's phenomenal growth during the 1980s and early 1990s. The growth of exports also appears to have been quite broad based, with a strong contribution from both small rural enterprises and foreign joint ventures: in Guangdong Province exports grew a remarkable 30 percent a year over the 1985–90 period but even in the rest of the country still expanded at the rate of 13 percent.[37]

There has also been a substantial shift in the composition of China's trade that seems more in line with its comparative advantage in labor-intensive products. Between 1980 and 1992 the share of

36. This comparison values GDP in dollars at the official exchange rate. See Bell, Khor, and Kochhar (1993, pp. 62–64).

37. Lardy (1992, p. 710).

primary materials in exports fell from 50 to 20.1 percent. The growth of exports is concentrated in industrial materials and light manufactures, principally apparel.[38] At a more detailed level, there is a strong inverse correlation between the growth of exports between 1985 and 1990 and the ratio of capital to labor used in production.[39] On the import side, the share devoted to primary products declined and machinery increased. Imports of consumer goods were still only about 5 percent of imports in 1992, and China has a very large potential for the future import of agricultural products.[40] The rural reforms of the early 1980s were extraordinarily effective in reducing food imports, but rising incomes are likely to raise imports in the future. Yields in Chinese agriculture are already high by international standards, and future growth in food consumption will likely be covered through imports.[41] To date, a large proportion of the growth in total imports has been in components of export products.

As shown in table 2-3, China's trade appears to be quite broadly based with respect to regions of the world. The published statistics are distorted by the inclusion of Hong Kong, since much of that trade is transshipped to other countries, principally the United States. According to trade statistics of the United States, for example, imports from China in 1992 totaled $27 billion compared with the Chinese export figure of $9 billion.[42] Thus we used the import data of the industrial countries to raise the share of Chinese trade directed toward those countries and reduced the share allocated to Hong Kong. On this adjusted basis, China's exports to the United States have grown particularly rapidly; but the exports to Europe and Japan have also increased substantially. On the import side, the growth has been largest in goods from other countries of Asia.

The contribution of the export sector to China's growth has been large, but not as overwhelming as sometimes presented. The contri-

---

38. Lardy (1992) finds a significantly negative correlation across industries between the post-1985 growth in exports and the capital-labor ratio. The correlation is positive and insignificant for the pre-1985 period.

39. Lardy (1992, p. 699); World Bank (1994a, p. 9).

40. World Bank (1992, table 4.2).

41. Anderson (1990).

42. Similar inconsistencies exist for trade with Europe and Japan. While the importers' estimate of trade with China is far in excess of its figure for exports, the discrepancies are almost fully offset by the differences in reported trade between these countries and Hong Kong. The discrepancies on the import side of China's trade are far smaller.

Table 2-3. *Structure of China's External Trade, 1980–93*
Billions of U.S. dollars

Region	Exports, f.o.b.					Imports, c.i.f.				
	1980	*1985*	*1990*	*1992*	*1993*	*1980*	*1985*	*1990*	*1992*	*1993*
World total	18.1	27.3	62.9	85.5	91.6	19.5	42.5	53.9	81.8	103.6
Central Europe[a]	0.9	0.9	0.6	0.3	0.6	1.0	1.2	1.0	0.6	0.8
Former Soviet Union	0.2	1.0	2.0	2.7	3.1	0.3	1.0	2.2	3.9	5.9
Industrial Europe	2.7	2.9	11.0	17.0	19.1	3.3	7.1	9.7	11.6	16.9
United States and Canada	1.1	3.7	13.2	22.2	28.9	4.6	6.3	8.1	10.8	12.0
Japan, Australia, and New Zealand	4.3	6.3	11.4	15.9	19.7	6.4	16.5	9.1	15.6	25.5
Hong Kong	4.4	5.7	13.6	12.4	2.1	0.6	4.8	14.6	20.5	10.5
Other Asia	2.2	3.6	6.4	9.5	11.6	1.1	2.3	6.0	13.5	25.4
Rest of world	2.4	3.3	4.7	5.5	6.4	2.2	3.2	3.2	5.3	6.5

Source: IMF (1994b). The export data for the industrial countries and Hong Kong have been adjusted for trade that passes through Hong Kong. The magnitude of this trade is estimated as the difference between China's reported exports to the industrial countries and their reported imports. Imports of the industrial countries were reduced by 10 percent to convert to f.o.b., and 25 percent of the difference was attributed to a trade margin added to goods that pass through Hong Kong. The adjustment was added to China's reported exports to the industrial countries, and deducted from its exports to Hong Kong.

a. Central Europe is defined as Bulgaria, the Czech and Slovak Republics, Hungary, Poland, and Romania.

bution to GDP growth for selected periods from 1980 to 1992 is shown in table 2-4. Exports have grown at twice the rate of the economy as a whole, but because the share of exports in GDP was very low in the beginning, the contribution to overall growth was initially quite low. As the share of the export sector in GDP expanded, it steadily became more important, but the domestic economy also participated in the acceleration of growth during the reform period. The size of the export sector in the total economy is greatly overstated because of the undervaluation of the currency. If GDP were measured on a PPP basis, it would increase by a factor of three and the share of exports would be sharply reduced. Furthermore, two-thirds of China's exports of manufactured goods are based on the processing of imported goods, where the estimated domestic value added is only about 25 percent.

Although all of the provinces have experienced accelerated growth since 1980, the highest growth rates were achieved in those coastal

Table 2-4. *Contribution of Exports to China's Growth, 1980–92*
Billions of U.S. dollars

Item	1980	1985	1990	1992
Real GDP, 1990 prices	138.4	222.4	316.5	390.9
Real exports, 1990 prices	8.4	20.9	53.2	77.4
Export share of GDP	6.1	9.4	16.8	19.8
		1980–85	*1985–90*	*1990–92*
Real GDP[a]		10.0	7.3	11.1
Real exports[a]		20.0	20.5	20.6
Contribution of exports to growth[a]		1.2	1.9	3.5

Sources: World Bank (1994b, pp. 204–07); Bell, Khor, and Kochhar (1993).
a. Average annual percentage change.

provinces with the largest share of exports in total output. Thus, the export liberalization may have had a dynamic effect in promoting change that went beyond its direct contribution to GDP.

There have been equally significant changes on the financial side of China's foreign economic relations. A summary of its external capital transactions is provided in table 2-5. China reported current account surpluses in the 1990–92 period and experienced a significant buildup of its international reserve position, but preliminary reports show a deficit for 1993. The rapid growth of capital inflows is shown by net external financing, which rose from $6.6 billion in 1985 to $23.3 billion in 1992. This increase implies an annual resource inflow equal to about 5 percent of GDP. This inflow (largely measured by data from outside sources) is not fully reflected in the Chinese balance of payments, which shows a net resource outflow as measured by the current account surplus. Apparently, the volume of unrecorded capital outflows has been very large.[43]

Nearly half of the external financing is in the form of foreign direct investment, which has soared from about $3 billion a year in the late 1980s to $11 billion in 1992 and an estimated $25 billion in 1993. This is undoubtedly a severe overstatement of the net inflow because

43. The magnitude of the overall problem is indicated in the residual asset transactions line. In 1993, China reported a current account surplus of $6 billion and reduced its reserves by $2 billion, a net resource outflow of $8 billion. Yet external sources identify $23 billion of net external financing, an inflow. Thus there was an implied outflow of capital of $31 billion. About half of this net outflow can be identified in other transaction categories of the Chinese balance of payments, but the remainder is unaccounted for.

Table 2-5. *External Financing in China, 1985–92*
Billions of U.S. dollars

Category	1985	1986	1987	1988	1989	1990	1991	1992
Balance: goods and services	−12.6	−7.6	0.2	−4.1	−5.0	10.6	11.5	5.0
(+) Net factor income	0.9	0.2	−0.2	−0.1	0.3	1.1	0.9	0.3
(+) Private transfers	0.2	0.3	0.2	0.4	0.2	0.2	0.4	0.8
(=) Current account, excluding official transfers	−11.5	−7.2	0.3	−3.8	−4.5	11.9	12.9	6.1
(+) Reserve change (− = increase)	2.4	1.4	−4.7	−2.3	0.6	−11.6	−14.1	2.1
(+) Asset transactions, residual	2.5	−1.4	−6.0	−4.3	−3.7	−9.6	−13.0	−31.4
(=) Net financial balance	−6.6	−7.2	−10.4	−10.4	−7.6	−9.2	−14.2	−23.3
Net external financing	6.6	7.2	10.4	10.4	7.6	9.2	14.2	23.3
(−) Official transfers	0.1	0.1	−0.0	0.0	0.1	0.1	0.4	0.4
(−) Direct investment	1.7	1.9	2.3	3.2	3.4	3.5	4.4	11.2
(−) Portfolio equity	0.0	0.0	0.0	0.0	0.0	0.0	0.7	1.2
(=) Net external borrowing	4.8	5.2	8.1	7.2	4.1	5.6	8.8	10.6
IMF credits	0.0	0.7	−0.1	−0.1	−0.1	−0.5	−0.5	0.0
Short-term debt	0.8	−0.3	2.1	0.6	−1.9	−0.1	3.5	0.5
Long-term debt	4.0	4.9	6.0	6.7	6.0	6.3	5.7	10.0
Amortization	−1.3	−1.9	−2.0	−2.3	−2.4	−3.4	−4.3	−5.2
Official creditors	1.2	1.4	1.1	1.8	2.8	2.6	2.7	3.1
Multilateral	0.6	0.6	0.7	1.1	1.2	1.2	1.5	1.5
Bilateral	0.6	0.8	0.4	0.7	1.6	1.4	1.2	1.6
Private creditors	4.1	5.3	6.9	7.2	5.7	7.1	7.3	12.1
Addenda								
Total debt	16.7	23.7	35.3	42.4	44.8	52.6	60.9	69.3
Percentage of GDP	5.7	8.5	11.6	11.2	10.5	14.2	16.3	16

Sources: IMF (1994a); World Bank (1994b).

it is believed that substantial amounts of domestic funds are being recycled through Hong Kong in order to take advantage of the large tax concessions provided to foreign investors.

China's total external debt reached about $70 billion in 1992, rising from 5.7 percent of GDP in 1985 to 16 percent in 1992. Yet that is still low in comparison with the economies of Central Europe and those of most other developing countries. All but about $10 billion of the debt is a long-term obligation. One-third is from official sources, and the rest from private lenders. China joined the World Bank and the International Monetary Fund in 1980. By the early 1990s, it had become the largest borrower from the World Bank, with an outstanding debt of $8 billion at the end of 1992 and new loan commitments of $3.2 billion in 1993. Japan has been by far the largest supplier of bilateral assistance, averaging $1–2 billion per year since 1988.[44] China has also become an active borrower in international bond markets, and outstanding bond issues have averaged about $5 billion in recent years.[45]

Future Steps

To date, the incremental nature of China's reform process has been very effective, but the distortions induced by the partial nature of the reforms are becoming more costly and are posing a threat of macro-economic instability. The distortions are particularly evident in foreign economic relations. As mentioned earlier, much of China's trade is of a shallow nature and involves the reprocessing of imported goods with a low level of value added. The import regime lacks transparency and fails to treat foreign firms uniformly. The tariff structure is relatively high and variable across product lines; and when it is combined with licensing and direct controls, the effective rates of protection are highly distortionary.[46]

Much of the reported foreign investment in China also appears to be a recycling of domestic funds to take advantage of the tax concessions granted to investments in the special enterprise zones. If the large amounts of foreign direct investment were reflective of a net inflow of capital, China would have some combination of a large trade deficit, reserve accumulation, and an appreciating real exchange rate, none of which is evident at present. Instead, the inflow of foreign direct investment appears to be matched by an unrecorded outflow of private capital.

Because the government has failed to reform the domestic tax system more rapidly and thereby provide a stable revenue base, it depends on the inflow of deposit funds to banks to finance its deficit and that of the state enterprises. That dependency will make it difficult to progress very far in liberalizing the domestic financial system

44. Lardy (1994, pp. 50–58).
45. World Bank (1993d, p. 91).
46. Some estimates of effective rates of protection on specific products are provided in World Bank (1994a, p. 71).

and allowing the entry of foreign financial firms to compete with the state in financial intermediation.

China has indicated a strong desire to rejoin GATT, and its membership has emerged as the next important step in integrating China more completely within the global trading system, but this measure will not work well without a considerable consolidation of past reforms in the trade area. China needs to reduce the role of administrative controls in favor of tariffs before it can comply with standard GATT conditions. Furthermore, it could reduce the distortions by adopting a more uniform tariff structure. The current administrative system governing imports is exceedingly complex and lacks the transparency needed to ensure that foreign firms are treated fairly. Once the domestic price liberalization is completed and the price of energy, in particular, is allowed to rise toward world market levels, this consolidation of trade reforms will be greatly simplified.

At the beginning of 1994 China took a large step toward unifying the exchange rate system by moving to a single rate based on a nationwide market. It now meets the basic conditions for current account convertibility with respect to its exchange rate system. It has not undertaken any significant degree of liberalization, however, that would allow foreign finance and service companies to participate in the domestic economy. Instead, it relies on Hong Kong to act as its primary agent in commercial dealings with other countries. As a result, finance and business services in Hong Kong have expanded rapidly and have provided considerable assistance to the tradables sector. This arrangement has been costly to the domestic economy, which has had to forgo the opportunity to use foreign technology and management skills as part of a broader modernization program. It also explains in part why China's trade links with the global economy have been shallow and why external trade has failed to spread widely beyond the area around Hong Kong. Although China should not attempt capital account convertibility, it could expand the involvement of foreign firms in finance and business services.

The most significant institutional issue to arise in the past few years concerns the renewal of China's membership in GATT. In broad terms, the Chinese trade regime is as open as that of some GATT members, and the more significant problems of admission to GATT are political, not economic, in nature. The earlier pattern of seeking to reform Chinese trade through negotiations with the United States has become excessively confrontational and interferes with other bilateral issues. Many of the conflicts with China over its policies toward trade, intellectual property rights, and services could be addressed within the multilateral framework of the World Trade Organization. This is particularly true now that the new GATT covers trade in services and intellectual property rights.

Conclusion

Over the past decade China has taken enormous steps toward integration with the global economy. In addition to increasing its own exports, it has emerged as an important market for other countries. It has also gained access to international capital markets on a large scale. This success seems all the more remarkable in that it was achieved through a series of external reforms that were widely criticized by Western economists for their gradual and partial character.

In achieving this expansion into world markets, China has benefited greatly from the assistance of overseas Chinese, something not available to the other transitional economies. Hong Kong has played a particularly important role as an intermediary for China's trade with the rest of the world. Trade between China and Hong Kong, and to a lesser extent between China and Taiwan, has been greatly expanded, but about 90 percent of that trade is for reexport. Furthermore, some of the reprocessing of imports for reexport represents the movement of plants a few miles across the border between Hong Kong and China to take advantage of lower labor costs.

Liberalization of the external sector has played a pivotal role in the accelerated pace of China's economic growth since 1980. It is evident, however, that the reforms in the domestic economy—particularly those that affected the rural sector—were of even greater importance, and China is more than just a case of export-led growth. In drawing lessons for other transitional economies from the Chinese experience, it is important to view the opening of the external sector in conjunction with the process of internal reform. That opening has been part of a broad program of liberalization, and it was undertaken in a process that seems strongly tailored to China's own unique economic and political situation.

To date, China's integration with the global economy has been of the shallow form, with an emphasis on the expansion of trade in goods and efforts to obtain some external financial assistance. Foreign firms are not significantly involved in the domestic economy, and China's finance, distribution, and service sectors—areas of increasing interest in recent international negotiations—remain by and large closed to outsiders. At the same time, the global economy has accepted a rapid expansion of China's trade, despite the appearance of many nontariff barriers. Rather than adopt internal institutions modeled after those of other countries, China has sought integration by using businesses in Hong Kong as an interface between it and the global economy. This works well at the level of trade in goods but will be less effective for trade in services.

In looking ahead, it is important to remember that, despite its enormous population, China remains a poor country with a limited impact on the global economy. The dollar value of its external trade is on a par with that of South Korea, a country with 4 percent of China's population. China's integration into the world economy has proceeded at a remarkably rapid pace, but it remains conspicuous in its exclusion from GATT. The lack of membership does not appear to have inhibited trade, but it does impart a significant degree of instability because China is outside the system for resolving multilateral trade disputes and thus is vulnerable to the vagaries of bilateral negotiations—principally with the United States. But that exclusion also means that it is not subject to the normal rules governing trade practices.

Chapter 3

The Former Soviet Union and the Russian Federation

*T*HE FIFTEEN independent states that replaced the same number of Soviet socialist republics at the end of 1991 share a similar heritage. All were subject to Soviet rule for anywhere from forty to seventy years, and all inherited the Soviet economic and political system. Indeed, for practical purposes they were integral parts of a single political and economic entity, and they had very close and intensive "trade" and other economic relationships within the Soviet Union. As part of the Soviet Union, they also had socialist-type trade relations with other socialist countries in Eastern Europe and Southeast Asia, mostly the members of COMECON (Council for Mutual Economic Assistance), and to some extent with developing economies and the West. Because of Russia's general leadership position and the concentration of all trade in the hands of the Soviet trade monopoly, however, their direct involvement in foreign trade was limited.

Nonetheless, the fifteen states differ in many other respects: in geographical location, cultural heritage, size, natural resources, degree of economic development, industrial structure, and the educational level of their populations (table 3-1). The extent of economic development and the structure of the economy of each state is an outcome of its own heritage, along with the Soviet government's economic policy toward it. This policy promoted intensive growth and increased economic dependence on the union; and it included efforts to Russify the other republics through the immigration of Russians and the imposition of the Russian culture.

Following the disintegration of the Soviet Union, these states faced a future of dramatic change. All professed a desire to move toward an

Table 3-1. *Former Soviet States: Basic Indicators*
1990 except where indicated

Republic	Population (millions)	GDP 1988, percent of total	GNP per capita, PPP U.S. = 100 1987	GNP per capita, PPP U.S. = 100 1991	Life expectancy at birth	Specialists with high education per 10,000	Manufacturing share (percent) GDP	Manufacturing share (percent) Labor force	Agriculture share (percent) GDP	Agriculture share (percent) Labor force
Russia	148.7	61.1	35.2	31.3	69	589	55	42	20	13
Ukraine	52.0	16.2	25.7	23.4	70	569	51	40	30	20
Kazakhstan	16.8	4.3	23.0	20.3	69	464	37	32	42	23
Belarus	10.3	4.2	29.7	31.0	71	627	54	42	28	20
Uzbekistan	20.9	3.3	12.1	12.6	69	386	39	24	44	39
Azerbaijan	7.1	1.7	20.2	16.6	71	455	47	26	38	32
Georgia	5.5	1.6	24.7	16.6	73	643	46	30	37	26
Lithuania	3.7	1.4	29.4	24.4	71	623	47	41	33	19
Moldova	4.4	1.2	23.1	21.0	69	476	43	30	42	33
Latvia	2.6	1.1	37.2	34.1	69	607	59	41	22	16
Armenia	3.4	0.9	24.3	20.8	72	623	71	42	17	18
Kyrgyzstan	4.5	0.8	14.2	14.8	66	417	44	28	43	33
Tajikistan	5.5	0.8	11.9	9.9	69	343	41	22	43	43
Turkmenistan	3.8	0.8	17.3	16.0	66	363	34	21	37	42
Estonia	1.6	0.6	45.8	36.6	70	643	61	43	20	13

Sources: Columns (1), (3)–(5): World Bank (1993e). Column (2): Fischer (1993, table 1). Column (6): Easterly and Fischer (1993, background material). Columns (7)–(10): World Bank (1993a).

open market economy. The more developed states have a large but distorted industrial structure and thus will have to concentrate on restructuring, but the less developed ones may be able to proceed along a more normal path of economic growth. The small states will be more dependent on the global market than the larger ones, including Russia; and those with some experience in international cooperation and trade will have an advantage. Those that are richer in energy and other natural resources in great demand will find it easier to finance the transition.

The nature and pace of the transition will also depend on the commitment of the political leaders to reform, their professional ability to carry it out, and the political support of the electorate. Some states have chosen a radical approach, at least at the start; others have been moving more gradually; while still others have undertaken few changes, other than those imposed by the Russian reform of 1992 and by the disintegration of the union.[1]

Each of the states is also facing the task of building a new state and changing over from an autocratic regime, centered in Moscow, into an independent, more or less democratic government. Here, too, their historical heritage, the composition of the population, the ability to reach political consensus, and the quality of the leadership will determine whether the new states will be able to execute any kind of coherent policy. Some have managed to create strong and effective governments and cohesive societies, but others have become engulfed in external or internal armed conflicts, or sharp political divisions.

In addition, the transition will be greatly affected by the extent of the cooperation among the republics, particularly in their relations with Russia, and by their ability to join the global economy. All of the states were strongly affected by the liberalization of prices in Russia in January of 1992 and the ensuing inflation that spread throughout the former Soviet Union because they continued to use a common currency. All also suffered from the disintegration of the trade network and the overnight conversion of a large volume of what had been internal trade into external trade. As a result of these actions, their first priority was to restore order in their monetary and external trade systems.

Each state will have to decide the extent to which it wants to cooperate with the others. Most had already decided to leave the

1. De Melo, Denizer, and Gelb (forthcoming a).

monetary union that was created by default following the disintegration of the USSR. However, ideas about a free-trade area, a CIS economic area, joint payment arrangements, or some other form of trade regime have been discussed. Russia in particular, a source of net aid flows to almost all other states under the old regime, will have to decide whether it wishes to continue a close association and under what conditions.

Although the other states initially moved to separate themselves from Russia as fast as possible, nearly all seem to be shifting back toward a preference for more cooperation. The Russians, who at first resented the move toward full independence of the other states, then grew ambivalent about it: they certainly wanted to preserve their political dominance but not to shoulder the economic burden that was involved. With the passage of time, Russia has been raising the price to the others of closer cooperation.

Since Russia accounts for more than half the population and GNP of the region, not to mention most of the military power and political leadership, it will undoubtedly play a pivotal role in the process of economic reform there. If Russia has a successful transition and can restore economic growth, the results will project to the other states and increase the level of cooperation. For some states, Russia may even become a sort of bridge with the global economy. By contrast, negative developments in Russia will further push the other states to search out their own independent paths.

Between 1991 and the end of 1993 all of the states suffered deep declines in production and high inflation rates, as well as sharp declines in trade volumes (table 3-2). These events were the outcome of their common heritage, the repressed inflation and dislocation created by the partial reforms of the Gorbachev era up to 1991, the negative consequences of the disintegration of the union (especially the decline in trade), and the aftermath of the Russian big-bang price liberalization of January 1992.

However, the rates of output and price change and their pattern varied markedly from one state to another. On the whole, production and trade declined most and inflation rates were highest in states with external or internal armed conflicts: Armenia, Azerbaijan, Georgia, Tajikistan, and Moldova. Sharp initial declines in production and trade and high rates of inflation were also experienced by Estonia, Latvia, and Lithuania, which had implemented early radical reforms

Table 3-2. *Changes in GDP and Inflation, Republics of the Former Soviet Union, 1991–94*

Republic	GDP (annual percentage change)				Inflation (annual rate)			
	1991	1992	1993	1994[a]	1991	1992	1993	1994[a]
Russia	−13.0	−19.0	−12.0	−12.0	93	1,353	915	336
Ukraine	−11.9	−17.0	−14.2	−25.0	91	1,210	4,735	1,000
Kazakhstan	−13.0	−14.0	−12.0	−6.0	91	1,381	1,571	1,680
Belarus	−1.9	−11.0	−11.6	−17.1	84	969	1,188	1,621
Uzbekistan	−0.9	−9.6	−2.4	−10.1	105	528	851	1,349
Azerbaijan	−0.7	−26.8	−13.3	−6.0	106	616	833	1,281
Georgia	−20.6	−42.7	−39.1	−10.0	78	913	3,126	10,000
Lithuania	−13.1	−37.7	−16.5	+4.7	225	1,020	410	69
Moldova	−18.1	−20.6	−14.8	−2.2	162	1,276	688	245
Latvia	−8.3	−33.8	−11.7	+4.1	124	951	109	36
Armenia	−11.8	−52.4	−14.8	+3.0	100	825	3,732	5,458
Kyrgyzstan	−5.0	−19.1	−16.0	−5.5	85	855	1,209	299
Tajikistan	−8.7	−30.0	−27.6	−15.0	112	1,157	2,195	1,500
Turkmenistan	−4.7	−5.3	−7.6	+1.7	103	493	3,102	1,608
Estonia	−11.3	−17.0	−2.1	+6.0	211	1,069	89	47

Source: IMF (1994f, table 11).
a. Estimated.

(not so radical in Lithuania) and had suffered most from the separation from Russia. In these countries, however, the collapse of output eased during 1993, and Estonia may record positive growth in 1994. The three Baltic countries also experienced higher initial rates of inflation, but with a substantial slowing after 1992.[2]

Average declines in output, also decelerating in the most recent year, were registered in Russia and Kazakhstan, which had both instituted moderate reform efforts. In these states the rate of inflation started to decline only during 1994. Finally, initial low declines in production were registered in states that had postponed serious reform: Belarus, Azerbaijan, Ukraine, and Uzbekistan. But they accelerated later in the period. Some of them, most notably Ukraine (but also the central Asian states), continue to experience very high rates of inflation. Turkmenistan, which started to exploit its vast gas reserves early on, stands out with the smallest decline in output and a resumption of growth in 1993.

2. Further details are provided in De Melo, Denizer, and Gelb (forthcoming a).

Table 3-3. *Changes in International and Interrepublic Trade Volume,*
1991–93
Annual percent

| | International trade | | | Interrepublic trade | | |
Republic	1991	1992	1993	1991	1992	1993
Russia	−40	−20	−2	−27	−22	−35
Ukraine	−32	−70	−8	−21	−19	−37
Kazakhstan	−26	−47	−17	−18	+5	−32
Belarus	−58	−50	−19	−26	−23	−20
Uzbekistan	−8	−45	−8	−31	−51	−7
Azerbaijan	−19	−37	−46	−19	−51	−50
Georgia	−75	−16	−8	−50	−67	−9
Lithuania	−63	−68	+81	−40	−39	−56
Moldova	−54	−61	+9	−44	−41	−18
Latvia	−69	+41	−6	−44	−55	−69
Armenia	−6	−85	−16	−37	−53	−41
Kyrgyzstan	−42	−82	+51	−15	−49	−45
Tajikistan	−11	−79	+162	−32	−70	−46
Turkmenistan	+6	+123	+65	−13	+3	−30
Estonia	−68	+95	+118	−35	−61	−48

Source: Michalopoulos and Tarr (1994, tables 1.1, 1.2). Trade flows are measured in U.S. dollars.
The conversion is based on implicit exchange rates, taking into account actual prices at which goods
were traded when different from world market prices (Belkindas and Dikhanov, 1994).

The decline in trade, both among the states of the former Soviet
Union and with the rest of the world, has been even more dramatic
than the decline in output (table 3-3).[3] By 1993, external trade,
measured in U.S. dollars, had declined by more than half, with most
of the fall occurring during 1991 and much of it in CMEA trade.
Trade among the states dropped even more sharply, both in volume
and value. Reduced Russian energy supplies and rising energy prices
to the other states, along with Russia's insistence on balancing trade
flows, were the principal factors behind this collapse. The most extreme declines took place in trade with the Baltic states, which were
trying to reorient their trade toward the West.[4] Although the internal

3. Because of extreme changes in relative ruble prices and in exchange rates, as well as
the problems of reporting trade flows, these data are of questionable quality. The general
trends, however, are quite clear. See Belkindas and Dikhanov (1994) for further discussion
of the problems in measuring trade flows. Additional data on trade flows are provided in
appendix table 3A-1.
4. Based on IMF (1994e); PlanEcon (1994b, p. 8); Fischer and Gelb (1991); Kirmani,
Enders, and Corsepius (1994); Michalopoulos and Tarr (1994, tables 1.1 and 1.2).

trade continued to fall in 1993, the drop in external trade appeared to bottom out for most of the republics. The Baltic states and a number of energy producers, notably Turkmenistan, managed to increase their exports and imports in 1993.

These statistics provide some insight into the magnitude of the problems involved in integrating the new states of the region into the global economy. The problems clearly extend far beyond those of at-the-border or shallow integration, which have more or less been resolved in the more developed parts of the world. In addition to establishing simple current-account convertibility, these states need to develop the institutional and service infrastructure required for foreign trade. More fundamentally, they need to change the composition of production, a change that will eventually define a new profile of comparative advantage for these countries.

While the rest of the world is contemplating integration of the deep variety—through the liberalization of trade in services and the coordination of internal regulations—the states of the former Soviet Union are struggling to create, almost from scratch, the *internal* institutional, service, and regulatory structures required by their infant market economies. Although their goal is much harder to accomplish, this is probably a unique opportunity to tailor these countries' internal institutions to the future demands of the global market. A well-functioning internal market is one of the most important conditions for effective participation in the international economy. A cliché from the early period of economic reform in the Soviet Union, sometimes attributed to Mikhail Gorbachev, states that before the country can embark on establishing an externally convertible currency it should create an internally convertible one. Thus far in the transition, the losses incurred from barriers and inefficiencies in internal trade are probably larger than those caused by less-than-optimal external trade. Although progress has been made on this front, many barriers, disruptions, and distortions are yet to be removed.

Common Problems

It is important to remember how many of the institutions that Westerners take for granted in considering the behavior of a market economy do not exist in the former Soviet states or are still in their infancy. These states are more extreme than those of Central Europe and China in the extent to which they had implemented the elements of a socialist state, their reliance on central planning, and the absence, before 1990, of any preparatory work to develop the foundations of a market-based economy. They also have operated under a socialist system far longer than the other socialist countries and previously had little or no experience with markets. All of these factors profoundly affect people's attitudes toward economic issues and their readiness for economic reform.

The Absence of Real Markets and the Collapse of Trade

With the onset of economic reform in the early 1990s, central planning was abolished, economic decisionmaking shifted to enterprises, prices were liberalized, and trade was freed to varying degrees. The most notable response to these changes was a collapse in the volume of trade at all levels: internal, interstate, CMEA, and international (which included trade with the West). It collapsed for a number of reasons. To begin with, new rules and regulations, new institutions, and distribution networks were not ready. Also, the old monopolistic system of distribution had persisted, and new monopolies were emerging.[5] There were sharp changes in the structure of demand (fewer government and enterprise orders for military production and for investments). And relative prices had undergone radical changes.

DOMESTIC TRADE. In addition, many new barriers to trade were imposed by local governments seeking to maintain low prices for various goods and services consumed locally, or seeking higher prices for goods produced in their territories and sold to others. Since the previous supply network had paid scant attention to considerations of location and distance, many supply links now crossed several administrative borders and covered quite long distances, greatly increasing the potential for disruption when regulations were no longer coordinated from the center.

In Russia and the other large republics, the initial decline in domestic trade probably inflicted the greatest damage on the level of production, more than that caused by the decline in interstate, CMEA, or international trade. For these states, then, the restoration

5. Brown, Ickes, and Ryterman (1993).

of freely flowing internal trade is the most urgent action required on the trade front. This is less true of the smaller states, which are more dependent on external trade, particularly for supplies of energy and other raw materials.

The former Soviet states were ill prepared to take advantage of the union's large market when the radical reform erupted at the beginning of 1992; and although matters have improved in some respects, they have deteriorated in others.[6] The improvements are mostly due to the gradual development of new commercial structures alongside or in place of the old state networks of wholesale and retail trade, and to the gradual withdrawal of official state trade. Even so, the domination of markets by local trade monopolies is declining only slowly, and in some cases they are being replaced by "Mafia"-type organizations with equally strong monopolistic powers. Initially, freer trade was achieved primarily by circumventing the existing networks and stores rather than by privatizing them. As a result, the cities of Russia were flooded with sidewalk "kiosks," while the spacious stores behind them remained empty of both goods and customers. Privatization of the retail stores and competition in the wholesale sector have stepped up since then, expediting trade and providing it with a much better infrastructure. Yet, many of the privatized stores and chains are moving rather slowly toward modern ways of marketing.

Another obstacle to free internal trade, more pronounced in Russia and the other large states, has been the rising political and economic power of different levels of local government: autonomous republics, oblasts, cities, and smaller administrative units. This general decentralization of power has its advantages, but it has also caused some setbacks in terms of helping to create a national market. One problem is that the regions negotiate separate deals with the central government regarding export rights, tax collection and sharing, and other special arrangements. Even worse, they enact their own laws and impose their own taxes, raise trade barriers of various kinds along their borders, and negotiate intergovernmental barter deals with their counterparts. All this helps to fracture and segment the national market. Although the decline in internal trade is undoubtedly part of a necessary adjustment—to eliminate obsolete production—the new

---

6. On the heritage of monopolization of trade and segmentation of markets, see Brown, Ickes, and Ryterman (1993); and Government of the Russian Federation (1993).

Table 3-4. *Total and Interrepublic Trade of the Republics of the Former Soviet Union*

Republic	Total trade (pereent)		Interrepublic trade, percent of total trade		Trade balance, world prices, percent of NMP, 1988
	NMP (1988)	GNP (1990)	1988	1990	
Russia	26.6	18.3	67.7	60.6	8.0
Ukraine	45.8	29.0	85.4	82.1	-2.8
Kazakhstan	33.8	47.3	91.4	86.8	-24.4
Belarus	76.1	28.5	91.5	89.4	-8.0
Uzbekistan	50.5	23.5	85.5	88.7	-12.1
Azerbaijan	62.3	28.9	94.2	85.9	-4.5
Georgia	57.6	33.9	93.2	87.7	-18.6
Lithuania	66.9	45.5	91.0	89.7	-41.5
Moldova	65.5	33.0	94.8	87.7	-33.4
Latvia	69.8	41.4	91.8	88.6	-18.4
Armenia	65.1	32.3	97.8	85.7	-24.0
Kyrgyzstan	51.4	35.9	97.7	86.5	-20.9
Tajikistan	48.7	28.4	85.8	90.1	-22.4
Turkmenistan	54.9	35.6	92.3	92.5	0.3
Estonia	73.9	32.9	90.0	91.6	-33.2

Sources: Columns (1), (3), (5): Fischer (1993, table 4). Columns (2), (4): World Bank (1993b, table 3.1). Trade is defined as exports plus imports.

trade barriers have contributed greatly to the fall in output. Even now, the expansion of internal trade would produce vast benefits, despite the fact that the goods might be of lower quality than those in the world market.

INTERREPUBLIC TRADE. The importance of trade among the republics, and the damage caused by its decline, is highlighted by the data of table 3-4.[7] In 1988 trade among the republics, which until 1991 in most cases was internal in every respect, represented 40 percent or more of net material product (NMP). In Ukraine and Kazakhstan it was about one-third. Only in Russia was trade with other republics a "low" 18 percent of NMP. If measured by world prices, these proportions would be even higher.

The available data suggest that interstate trade fell even more sharply than internal trade, roughly by 50 percent between 1990 and 1992. It was hampered not only by the lack of appropriate trade

7. Christensen (1994); Brown and Belkindas (1993).

institutions, such as clearing mechanisms and border stations, but also by numerous disputes over prices. Energy prices were still under state control, and the prices of many goods traded between republics were loaded with transfer elements, usually a net transfer from Russia to the other republics, as explained below.[8]

CMEA TRADE. The third main channel of trade under the functional autarky of old was with the CMEA countries. This trade was conducted, supposedly at "world prices," via bilateral agreements between governments. As explained in chapter 1, the unit of account was the transferable ruble. Although it was used for all CMEA transactions, it never became an instrument of multilateral clearing. As also discussed later, it strongly favored the East European partners and served as a means of providing Soviet subsidies to these countries.

When the CMEA tried to trade with convertible currencies, it collapsed. Russia, which accounted for the vast bulk of that trade, reports that the value of CMEA trade fell from $66.3 billion in 1990 to $10.9 billion in 1993 (table 3-5). Nearly all of the decline occurred in 1991. Although the drop in imports had some disruptive effects on Russian output because of supply bottlenecks, many of the exports affected were energy products that could be resold elsewhere for hard currencies. Thus, the benefits to Russia of reduced subsidy payments may have offset the costs of the supply disruptions.

TRADE WITH THE WEST. The fourth channel of trade was with the rest of the world, both developing and developed countries. Most of the trade with developing economies was conducted through bilateral agreements, in a mixture of soft and hard currencies. Trade with the industrial countries and a few other trade partners was conducted in hard currencies, and at world market prices. Like all other external trade, however, it was handled by the Soviet trade monopoly and in many cases within the framework of bilateral trade agreements.

The Soviet monopoly of foreign trade, together with the state price committees, set the domestic ruble prices of imported goods at levels that had little or no relation to CMEA or world prices, and producers of exported products were paid the domestic prices. The differences between domestic prices and CMEA or world prices were collected (or paid) as foreign trade taxes. Since the official rate of exchange was

8. Additional information and estimates of the magnitude of the subsidy are provided in Bofinger and Gross (1992, table 2); Werner (1993, table 2); Brown and Belkindas (1993).

Table 3-5. *Russian Federation Trade with Countries outside the Former Soviet Union, 1980–93*
Billions of U.S. dollars

Region	1980	1985	1990	1991	1992	1993
Exports						
Total	49.6	72.5	80.9	60.0	41.6	43.9
Former CMEA countries[a]	24.3	40.1	34.8	12.2	8.3	7.7
China, Korea, Lao P.D.R., former Yugoslavia	2.6	4.2	b	b	b	b
Developed countries[c]	15.9	18.6	30.3	37.2	25.4	26.6
Developing countries[d]	6.9	9.6	15.8	10.6	7.9	9.6
Imports						
Total	44.5	69.1	89.9	49.7	37.2	33.1
Former CMEA countries[a]	21.4	37.6	34.8	11.1	5.4	3.8
China, Korea, Lao P.D.R., former Yugoslavia	2.2	4.6	b	b	b	b
Developed countries	15.7	19.3	32.4	30.9	22.9	18.3
Developing countries	5.1	7.6	15.7	7.7	8.9	11.1

Sources: IMF (1991, p. 107; 1980; 1985); Michalopoulos and Tarr (1994, table 1.5); authors' calculations.

a. Includes Bulgaria, Cuba, Czech and Slovak Republics, Hungary, Mongolia, Poland, Romania, and Vietnam.

b. Included in developing countries for 1990.

c. OECD for 1990–93.

d. "Rest of the World" for 1990–93.

extremely overvalued, large sums were collected as import "taxes." Following the rise in world energy prices in the early 1970s, there was also a large price differential on energy products, the main Soviet export to the West. Thus although Soviet trade with the nonsocialist world expanded rather rapidly after 1960s, it did little to relax the autarkic trade regime of the Soviet Union.

The Distorted Composition of Production and Comparative Advantage

The socialist composition of internal production and the biases and gaps in the technology of production highly distorted the pattern of trade when compared with normal concepts of comparative advantage. The composition of both production and foreign trade was determined by the ministries that ruled over consumer sovereignty. The leadership's strategy was to devote more resources to investment and defense, and hence to heavy manufacturing, and fewer resources to private consumption, housing, and services. Because of these distortions, the creation of new institutions alone will not be enough to reform the foreign trade sector.

The old structure of production makes for a particularly difficult transition: the highest proportion of GNP was devoted to military goods and heavy manufacturing, both of which were probably over-concentrated in Russia. Among the republics, it had the largest share of basic industries and metalworking, heavy industry, and the producer goods industry; and the lowest share of manufacturing devoted to consumer goods.[9] The Soviet Union was a net importer of food, manufactured consumer goods, and machines and equipment, even from other socialist countries. It also had less experience with normal trade (especially in manufacturing) with the West than most of the East European economies. As a result, Soviet goods were technologically unable to compete on the world market.

Additional Distortions of the Old System

The Soviet Union was the most extreme example of functional autarky, as pointed out in chapter 1. Central planning almost completely eliminated internal and external economic competition as an efficiency-enhancing force. Because of the endemic shortages, competition on the marketing side was even weaker than that on the buying side. The gap caused by the lack of a competitive spirit for more than seventy years is probably the most difficult one to fill and may require the most external involvement.

At the beginning of the transition, the institutional and regulatory infrastructures needed to make competition work were entirely missing. These include a long list of market, financial, and business services, notably a market infrastructure for the conduct of external trade. Individual enterprises had no prior experience of operating in

9. Brown and Belkindas (1993). A number of other advanced countries in transition or individual republics may have had relatively larger sectors of machine building to balance the absence of any basic natural resources (for example, Belarus, Estonia, Czechoslovakia, Hungary, and Bulgaria).

the global market, and there was no network of foreign trade corporations to assist them. Even now, the private service sector remains
highly underdeveloped.

Before the new governments can perform the supporting and
regulatory role required of the administration in a market economy,
they will have to undergo some restructuring. One of the most difficult adjustments will be to distinguish between the old and the new
ways of intervening in the economy. Under the old system, government officials made the most important decisions, which in market
economies are made by the market. Now they must play a secondary,
mostly regulatory, role. Serious complications arise when the same
people who made the old decisions are entrusted with the new ones.
Indeed, during the early years of the transition, there has been a
decline in the ability of the government to govern, even to sustain the
level of normal government services, such as law enforcement and
public health. This general deterioration in governance has become
another obstacle to the transition.

Under the circumstances, the new regimes have found it especially
difficult to carry out one of the major responsibilities of government,
that is, to maintain macroeconomic stability. When prices are freed,
money takes on a new role, and the monetary overhang from previous
repressed inflations has to be eliminated. As a result, the government's exchange rate policy assumes a particularly decisive role in
controlling inflation. Being the only price that is perceived as "correct" in an environment of enormous change in the structure of
relative prices, the rate of exchange becomes a crucial nominal anchor
for the price system.

The rate of exchange and its role in the early stages of the transition
are also greatly affected by another prominent characteristic of the old
system: with limited exceptions, the only assets that private households were allowed to accumulate were nominal ruble savings (in the
form of savings accounts or government bonds paying low nominal
interest rates). The uncertainty and inflation of the transition eliminated, at least for a time, the domestic currency as a store of value. Yet
the creation of new assets—equity in firms and real estate—was
delayed by the slow pace of legislative changes and privatization. As a
result, foreign currency became the only legal and safe asset to hold.
The ensuing flight of capital caused the value of the ruble to plummet
far below any notion of an equilibrium rate, such as purchasing power

parity, with serious repercussions on the rate of inflation and on the development of foreign trade.

Whatever actions they take, the new republics cannot seem to escape the burden of their legacy: the extreme socialist structure of the Soviet Union. Restructuring, in the sense of changing the production mix, is therefore likely to be more difficult and prolonged for these states than for most other centrally planned economies. It will be equally hard for them to introduce privately operated personal and business services, including trade and financial services, and to create a market infrastructure. In these areas, international involvement—through trade, investment, and technical assistance, as well as some aspects of deep integration—can have substantial benefits.

In view of the magnitude of the distortions in prices and production, what is the optimal strategy for reforming the foreign trade regime? Can the shock of opening up and introducing the new set of relative prices do the job properly? Or will the old system have a lasting effect on the future structure of comparative advantage and trade patterns?

Russia

With more than half the population and the production capacity of the old Soviet Union, the Russian Federation is its natural continuation. Moscow, as the center of economic planning, had most of the old institutions dealing in foreign economic relations, including trading companies, banks, and experienced personnel. Thus the new foreign trade regime and policies of the Russian Federation will carry some weight among all the new republics. In this section we review the Russian experience with economic reform in the 1990–94 period, provide an account of the evolution of its foreign trade policies, and examine the options for the future.

Russia's Special Features

Of all the former Soviet republics, Russia had developed the most socialist structure of production and trade. It was the largest importer of food, consumer goods, and (light) machinery and a sizable exporter of raw materials and metals, heavy industry and machinery,

Table 3-6. *Russian Federation Trade with Countries outside the Former Soviet Union, by Product Group, 1990–92*
Estimates in percent of total

Product group	Exports			Imports		
	1990	1991	1992[a]	1990	1991	1992[a]
Machinery and equipment	18	10	10	41	33	38
Mineral and metal products	51	63	66	7	9	3
Oil and gas	43	42	54	. . .	. . .	. . .
Chemical products	4	6	7	4	9	10
Raw and processed food products	2	2	3	15	24	29
Other goods and services	20	13	14	29	20	20

Sources: Data obtained from Government of the Russian Federation (1994c); Konovalov (1994, table 2.6); IMF staff estimates.

a. 1992 data are not directly comparable with data for 1990–91 because of the change in classification from the material product system to the harmonized system.

and military goods (table 3-6). It continues to have the largest internal market—consisting of nearly 150 million people—and thus has the most to gain from converting to a market-based economy. With such a market, Russia could develop its own industries to meet the demand for consumer products and new producer goods. This market and the potential trade with other former Soviet states means that Russia depends to a lesser extent on trade with the global economy in reorganizing its own economy. It can achieve many of the necessary economies of scale through its large internal market, which also provides a basis for developing future export capability. Producers can accumulate experience in the production of new products and improve them in the internal market before moving outside. In many cases, significant exports need only emerge after the saturation of the internal market. Here, too, domestic producers can build up their competitive skills on the economic and technological front, a necessary condition for learning to compete externally.[10]

Since Russia has an abundant supply of energy and other natural resources—such as ferrous and nonferrous metals, timber, and chemicals—it has the potential to maintain a high level of natural resource exports, including some in semiprocessed form. Exports of these products will go a long way toward financing necessary

10. Porter (1990, chap. 3).

imports at a relatively high equilibrium rate of exchange. This is a great advantage, because it ensures adequate foreign exchange revenues over a prolonged period of transition to cover the import needs of modern technology and services, and to service foreign debts and foreign investments. A country with such natural resources can also attract foreign capital more readily, which can be directed mainly to the development of these resources in exchange for export earnings.

The great drawback in this otherwise advantageous position is that most Russian manufactured goods are still of a lower quality than that preferred by both the population and producers for imported manufactures. Consequently, it will be difficult to develop internal markets for these products. Under the current structure of Russia's comparative advantage, not to mention an open trading regime and low tariffs, large sections of the manufacturing sector will find themselves at a competitive disadvantage, and at risk of being seriously challenged by imports. Such competition will come from the industrial West, the newly industrializing economies of Asia (the NIEs), and from less developed countries, such as China.

To a certain extent, the Russian case resembles that of the oil-rich countries, which found themselves unable to develop significant manufacturing sectors because of an appreciated exchange rate. Russia, however, already has a large, albeit inefficient, manufacturing sector. This makes matters even worse in some respects. Like the other formerly centrally planned economies, Russia could make a case for some transitory protection from imports, to provide time for modernizing its industry. In the case of the Central European countries, that protection is likely to take the form of an initially depreciated exchange rate since they must export manufactured goods. For Russia, however, the short-term potential for natural-resource-based exports may lead to a more normal exchange rate that would place the manufacturing sector at a competitive disadvantage during its transition. Admittedly, this is not an immediate problem for Russia, since the exchange rate collapsed in the initial economic turmoil. But the question of the optimal degree of openness will become more relevant once Russia makes some progress in restoring macroeconomic stability and there is a recovery of the exchange rate, as discussed in a later section.

Internal and External Reforms, 1991–94

Thus far, reform has been uneven and extremely difficult to implement in Russia, primarily because the government failed to achieve macroeconomic stabilization following the price liberalization of January 1992. The foremost problem was the nearly complete lack of preparatory work prior to the reform measures or introduction of the reforms of 1991. The increasing but partial freedom of action granted to economic agents, combined with the deteriorating central control, particularly during 1991, merely accelerated the rate of open inflation and unleashed the repressed inflation. Shortages became more severe and widespread than ever, and excess money balances grew sharply, as most prices were still kept under state control. The year 1991 was also marked by political struggles on the nature of the reforms (hence the coup of August) and on the fate of the Soviet Union. Both added to the difficulties of implementing a coherent reform program. The actual dissolution of the union and the way it was done posed a large problem for the stabilization efforts of 1992 and thereafter.

The reforms at the beginning of 1992 under the Gaidar government were far more radical. Central planning was formally abolished and prices and wages were almost completely liberalized. At the same time, the ruble was made convertible for current account transactions. The foreign exchange price of the ruble was to be determined in an open daily auction, and foreign exchange became legal tender for internal transactions and saving purposes by both households and firms.

INTERNAL REFORMS. The liberalization of prices in January 1992 was accompanied by fiscal and monetary efforts to stabilize the economy, but these efforts were only partly successful and only for the first few months. Prices immediately soared 300–400 percent, which was much higher than anyone had projected (and more than the increase in the Central European countries). After a lull of a few weeks, a period of sustained and high inflation (at variable monthly rates of 10–30 percent) set in and continued until mid-1993. Beginning in the summer of 1993, the inflation rate was gradually reduced, to a monthly rate of about 5 percent by the middle of 1994, but it again picked up in the fall of 1994 (table 3-7).

Table 3-7. Dynamic of Russian Prices, Exchange Rates, and Wages

Date	CPI (June 1992 = 100)	Monthly inflation[a] (percent)	Nominal noncash exchange rate (rubles/$)	Real exchange rate (rubles/$; June 1992 = 100)	Nominal monthly wage (rubles)	Real wage (rubles; June 1992 = 100)[b]	Nominal monthly wage ($)
April 1991	7	...	32	357	400	128.6	12.5
January 1992	35	...	180	434	1,438	82.0	8.0
April 1992	75	30	155	173	3,024	78.7	19.5
July 1992	111	14	136	103	5,452	96.7	40.0
October 1992	116	15	338	173	8,853	104.1	26.2
January 1993	330	26	442	115	15,890	91.0	34.7
April 1993	589	21	779	114	30,562	102.5	39.2
July 1993	1,016	20	1,025	88	55,995	108.2	54.6
October 1993	1,889	23	1,093	56	93,000	96.7	85.1
January 1994	2,920	16	1,356	41	134,161	90.2	98.9
April 1994	3,770	9	1,787	42	171,500	89.3	96.0
July 1994	4,498	6	2,060	41	224,000	97.6	108.7
August 1994	4,678	4	2,197	42	232,800	97.6	106.0
September 1994	5,038	7.7	2,633	47	255,000	99.2	96.8
October 1994	5,632	11.8	3,075	48	273,000	92.7	88.8
November 1994	6,432	14.2	3,234	44	281,600	83.7	87.1
December 1994	7,487	16.4	3,560	42	...	...	...

Source: Government of the Russian Federation (1994b).

a. Prior to August 1994 the inflation rate is computed as the average of current and previous two months.

b. Corrected for inflation in the United States.

Several reports have commented on Russia's failure to stabilize the economy.[11] As they point out, the main problem was that Russia was unable to reduce the budget deficit and restrict the cheap credits and subsidies going to various sectors of the economy.[12] Rates of interest on central bank ruble credits and in the commercial sectors were extremely negative in real terms during 1992 and 1993, and only toward the end of 1993 did central bank policies and other restrictive efforts raise real interest rates to positive levels. The bizarre monetary union that prevailed among the former Soviet republics through 1992 and parts of 1993—under which a dozen or so independent central banks could issue ruble credits—also had an adverse effect, as did the continued subsidies and credits granted by Russia to the other former Soviet states. At least some of the deeper explanations for this failure are of a political nature, as reflected in the inability to build a political consensus for more radical action. Needless to say, restructuring the Russian economy was a horrendous task to begin with, but it was made all the worse by disagreements about the components of the stabilization package, the appropriate monetary and fiscal restraints, nominal controls of wages and the exchange rate, and restrictions on the use of foreign currency for internal transactions.

The government struggled constantly to bring the fundamentals into line with greater stability. It drastically reduced central bank credits in 1993 and again in 1994, and increased interest rates. It did narrow the budget deficit in a perfunctory way by limiting actual expenditures, even if authorized by the budget, but failed to get to the root of the problem. Some of these efforts were formalized in a new agreement on stabilization between Russia and the IMF in the spring of 1994, followed by a rescheduling of the Russian foreign debt and the granting of more international support. Unfortunately, the basic fiscal structure has shown only limited improvement so far. The rate of inflation has certainly begun to decline—in response to reduced credits to the other former Soviet states, the introduction of short-term government bonds to finance part of the budget deficit, and

11. See, for example, Sachs (1994b); Blejer (1993); Easterly and da Cunha (1994); Ofer (1994).

12. It is difficult to get meaningful estimates of the Russian budget deficits. The overall 1992 deficit was about 28 percent of GNP, more than half of it financed by foreign credits to Russian imports. During 1993 and in the preliminary data for 1994, the deficit stood at about 10 percent of GNP (Sachs, 1994b, tables 2–4, 7).

possibly some increase in the demand for rubles following a long period of escaping from it—but this trend is far from secured. Indeed, the pressures on the government to pay its budgetary obligations and to ease the new payment crisis that developed during 1994 are mounting. In September the inflation rate rose back to nearly 8 percent, and by year end it had reached 16.4 percent per month. The ruble was sharply devalued in early October, and the governor of the central bank resigned. Real and sustained stabilization still lies in the future for Russia, although it may be more likely than some have suggested.

The continued economic instability and political strife have seriously interfered with the creation of a freer and more smoothly functioning national market. Under conditions of high and variable inflation, trade and exchange are more difficult and risky; accounting, financing, and clearing are more complex; and new businesses are harder to establish. The unstable macroeconomic environment, the shaky financial sector, and the weak legal and enforcement agencies have, in combination, delayed the growth of small and medium-sized private firms and discouraged potential foreign investors. Equally worrying is the little advance, even retreat, in the area of governance. Although the legislative process is gradually improving, law enforcement and the quality of government services are not. Exemptions, corruption, and the frequent changing of rules have become commonplace.

However, significant progress has occurred in the privatization of enterprises. Almost all small businesses have been privatized, and many new ones have been established. Furthermore, the majority of large-scale enterprises have been privatized. According to official data, nearly 80 percent of all employees in industry were employed by private enterprises by the fall of 1994.[13] The privatization program, based on vouchers and auctions, was almost completed in the summer of 1994, and a new stage of direct cash sales is being prepared. The effects of privatization on the behavior of many of the large enterprises will only gradually become apparent because they were sold to their own workers and managers, and some continue to have access to soft credits. There are still enough monopolies to inhibit the growth of competition, and the Mafia remains very active. All the

13. Government of the Russian Federation (1994a, p. 7).

same, markets continue to become freer, relative prices are moving more in line with costs, and some restructuring toward the consumer industries and services is taking place.

In order to buffer the initial price shock, the government continued to control the prices of energy and some raw materials, intending to raise them periodically toward world levels. With inflation running higher than expected, the ruble collapsing, and political pressures mounting, however, the government has been unable to achieve that goal. Although key energy prices have moved closer to world levels, the persistent gap between domestic and world market prices has complicated efforts to reform the foreign trade regime.[14]

FOREIGN EXCHANGE REGIME. The price liberalization of January 1992 was followed by a gradual freeing of the rate of exchange. In a number of steps during 1992 the preexisting system of multiple exchange rates was unified, and the foreign exchange price of the ruble was determined in an open daily auction. Although the exchange rate was free to float according to market forces, the Central Bank of Russia maintained the power to intervene, an option that it has frequently used since the middle of 1992. The relatively free market for foreign currency played an important role in internal macroeconomic developments and in turn was strongly affected by them. The rate of exchange (the dollar price of the ruble) initially set by the government represented an extreme devaluation of the former official rates but was above the level in the "free," or gray market that existed at the end of 1991. Early in 1992 the ruble declined to less than 5 percent of the value consistent with purchasing power parity and in subsequent months (until October) continued to deteriorate, sometimes at slower, but usually at faster rates than the internal rate of inflation.

The main reason for the low external value of the ruble was that foreign currency was almost the only asset in the economy, liquid or otherwise, that could serve as a low-risk and stable store of value. Real

14. By the end of 1993, the price of crude oil was only 31 percent of the world market price, but that represented a doubling of the relative price compared with January 1992. The relative prices of coal and of natural gas did not change significantly over the year. Prices of oil products, such as gasoline, increased by more; and, by the end of 1993, they were between two-thirds and three-quarters of the world market prices (Government of the Russian Federation, 1993, pp. 50–51). Some further adjustment of domestic energy prices toward world market levels occurred during 1994. As of the beginning of 1995 there may be additional easing of quantitative controls and further increases in energy prices.

estate could not serve as a secure asset because Russia had no clear legislation on private property rights and still severely restricts sales of land. Prevailing negative real interest rates prevented the development of a serious bond market until late in 1993. Being internal legal tender, foreign exchange came into even greater demand as people and enterprises ran away from the ruble. Following the liberalization and inflation, there was a massive shift of private savings to hard currency: households and enterprises held more than half their financial deposits in foreign currencies.[15] At the end of 1992, dollar deposits were larger than the money supply (M2).[16] In addition, capital flight during 1992 was estimated at around $20 billion.[17]

In the last quarter of 1992, the rate of depreciation of the exchange rate began to lag behind inflation and the real exchange rate started to decline, a process that continued until September of 1994 (table 3-7). This change was sparked by a rise in the confidence of the population in the Russian economy, an improvement in the balance of payments and foreign exchange reserves, a gradual increase in the supply of alternative domestic assets, and a rise in domestic real interest rates. The privatization program, with its massive distribution of vouchers to the entire population, was initiated during this period. In 1993 Russia recorded a trade surplus of $14 billion—due in part to severely depressed domestic demand and unusually good agricultural harvests— and this trend continued in 1994. Similar benefits have followed from the March 1994 agreement with the IMF and from the debt-rescheduling agreement with the clubs of Paris and London in April and with private banks in October, which reduced pressures from creditor countries. These arrangements were more important than direct (other than debt relief) financial assistance from the West, which totaled $2.5 billion in 1993.[18] There are indications that capital flight has subsided, and some previously exported capital may be returning, together with some private investment.[19] Negotiations with GATT (the new WTO) concerning Russian membership are also in high gear. All of these positive developments allowed the central bank to

15. Fischer (1993).
16. Government of the Russian Federation (1993, table 11).
17. Foreign aid during 1992 was extremely small, excluding the financing through export credits of much of the massive Russian import subsidies. See Sachs (1994b, p. 56).
18. Sachs (1994b, p. 56). This excludes $5.5 billion in export credits.
19. "Investments in Russia," *New York Times,* October 5, 1994, p. A6)

stabilize the rate of exchange and smooth the short-run movements with modest interventions in the foreign exchange market. In the fall of 1994 the central bank appeared to have gone too far in protecting the ruble, and a significant depreciation took place during the last months of 1994.

TRADE REGIME. Despite the significant real appreciation of the exchange rate from its bottom levels during 1992, it was only about one-third of the PPP value in the fall of 1994. Thus for the entire period of transition Russian industry has benefited from a protective shield provided by the depreciated ruble and will no doubt continue to be protected for some time into the future. Note, too, that the average dollar wage in Russia was only $8 per month right after the onset of the reforms in 1992 but slowly rose over the next two years to reach more than $100 as of August 1994 (table 3-7). If trade were conducted at market exchange rates in this environment, exports would become extremely cheap and imports very expensive. When it is remembered that the domestic prices of a number of key exportable goods, mostly energy and raw materials, were kept artificially low by continued government controls, the pressures for government intervention in trade become clear. The result has been a very uneven process of trade liberalization.

In the late 1980s the Soviet government took a number of preliminary steps to ease the centralized mode of foreign trade. Beginning in 1987, it allowed a few major exporters to retain part of their foreign exchange earnings for import purposes and introduced a system of differentiated exchange rates to encourage exports. Government-run auctions in foreign exchange were introduced in 1989, but they were insignificant. On balance, these early Soviet reforms had largely negative effects. The volume of imported food and consumer goods increased sharply, and this, with the help of a number of external shocks, including declining terms of trade, caused the external debt to double over the next five years to $61 billion.[20]

In addition, as already noted, the political changes in Central Europe after 1989 disrupted trade in the CMEA, with significant effects on production. That decline was greatly exacerbated by the Soviet government's decision to abolish the traditional bilateral soft

---

20. Christensen (1994). On the development of Soviet and Russian debt through 1993, see World Bank (1993b, p. 139).

currency trade regime and to replace it with one based on hard currency starting in 1991. Similar consequences followed from the partial disruption of supply lines across republican borders; but the largest collapse of interstate trade occurred during 1992.

Since then Russia has also liberalized the trade regime, as part of the general reform program, but the changes have been less sweeping and comprehensive. Russia is interested in joining GATT (the new WTO), and many of the changes are part of the attempt to qualify.[21]

First, it abolished the state monopoly over foreign trade, and by January 1992 all firms were allowed to trade directly. However, state trading companies remained to take care of state needs and to manage trade in essential goods. In 1993 the government even reestablished a number of government export companies to control exports of several strategic goods. "Recontract," a remnant of the old state trade monopoly, is still large (half a million employees) and uses export quotas to centralize and cross-subsidize some exports and imports. The list of goods subject to centralized trade has declined, but the proportions within each category have increased. The trade monopoly is also an important revenue producer for the government, and any reduction in its role would have a significant fiscal effect while narrowing the differential between the domestic and foreign price. Such organizations also take part in executing bilateral agreements with the former Soviet states and a few other countries.

Second, Russia is following the general legislation of the European Union in setting up a system of customs administration, which includes trade codes, product classification, and standards. It is taking time to implement this system, however. The current legislation and regulations are still infested with detailed provisions for special treatment and exemptions of some products or enterprises. At this point, significant amounts of trade (especially across state borders) are unrecorded or falsely recorded, and the quality of the customs-based trade statistics is low.

However, a substantial volume of exports remains subject to restrictions of various kinds. As mentioned previously, some of these restrictions were necessitated by the extreme undervaluation of the ruble, which would have implied extraordinarily high domestic prices

21. A recent good summary of the main elements of the evolving Russian trade regime can be found in Konovalov (1994).

for some tradables, or by decisions to raise the price of some domestic products, such as energy and raw materials, to world levels only gradually. The government also sought to extract part of the windfall proceeds that would otherwise accrue to the enterprises. The initial export trade regime was a tangled system of taxes on foreign exchange earnings and requirements that part of these earnings be surrendered, initially at an inferior exchange rate and later at the established rate; of export quotas and licensing; and of export taxes. The system was made even more complex by widespread exemptions and special treatments.

This system is gradually moving toward more uniform taxes on industrial products and less licensing. The export quotas (only a small fraction of which were auctioned) were scheduled for elimination after May 1994, except for those classified as "state needs and obligations." That measure should reduce some of the distortions of relative prices and rent seeking, and it is expected to raise fiscal revenues.

Export taxes on oil, gas, and other raw materials had been high. They were imposed as specific taxes (in dollars per ton) and ranged up to 80 percent in value (about 30 percent on energy products). In addition there were surcharges on barter and joint venture deals, but with many exemptions and evasions. As of July 1994 the rates and the exemptions were reduced (by about half) in the hope of making collection more efficient. Under the new reforms, export taxes are intended to be a primary instrument to affect relative prices in Russia (but see the discussion on import taxes below). There are still restrictions on who can export "strategic goods," which of course act as a nonmonetary barrier. In January 1995 all formal quantitative restrictions on oil exports were removed and replaced by a uniform export tax. However, a committee is to allocate scarce pipeline capacity, a move that some see as potentially distorting the export quotas.

The export restrictions and taxes have been opposed by the affected industries for obvious reasons, but more recently some producers, such as the aluminum industry, have been arguing for protection against imports because of the rising real exchange rate. They claim that their production costs approach world prices, even though the ruble has remained highly undervalued from a PPP perspective. With the continued appreciation of the ruble, the number of industries that will be unable to export will increase. The more downstream processing industries will be particularly hard hit because they embody the inefficiencies of the old system to a greater extent.

On the import side, the unexpectedly large initial (1992) devaluation forced the government to introduce high subsidies to support the prices of imports of basic foods, medicines, and certain raw materials. Many firms continue to arrange for imports through central government organizations. The cost of these subsidies, up to 95 percent of the world prices in some cases, amounted to about 14–18 percent of GNP in 1992, and most were not included within the budget.[22] Since then the subsidies for basic imports have been phased out, except in a few cases such as medicine. The licensing for imports has also been reduced. Imports of less critical materials, however, have been subjected to increasing tariffs. A unified tariff law was first introduced in July of 1992 with a basic rate of 5 percent and four categories: a zero rate for former Soviet countries, 2.5 percent for developing countries, the general rate for most favored countries, and 10 percent for non-favored countries. A significant number of exceptions were subject to a higher rate, however.

These tariffs have been raised on several occasions, so that by the summer of 1994 the average rate was about 13 percent, and ten product groups qualified for tariffs of 100 percent. A law passed in January 1994 was supposed to eliminate all enterprise-specific exemptions, but it has yet to be tested in practice. In addition, there are differential excise taxes, on top of the 20 percent VAT, and special controls and other nontariff barriers have become increasingly common.[23]

These measures are a reflection of the pressures exerted on the government by domestic producers who feel threatened even at the present level of "natural" protection provided by the undervalued exchange rate. The pressures are growing despite the fact that the domestic costs of energy and a number of other basic materials remain at a fraction of world prices, the exchange rate is still only a third of its PPP rate, and the dollar wage is about $100 per month.[24] As domestic prices approach those of the world market and begin to reflect the underlying low efficiency and high cost of production, the

22. Christensen (1994).
23. On the development of taxes and barriers affecting imports and exports in Russia since 1992, see World Bank (1993b); Dyker (1993b); Werner (1993); Christensen (1994); Konovalov (1994).
24. World Bank (1993b, p. 25).

pressure to export products based on natural resources will ease somewhat, and the attraction of imports will rise. All these trends point to a possible decline in the competitive advantage of many Russian manufactures.

In summary, the initial wave of inflation, devaluation, and declining production and trade has been both more severe and longer lasting in Russia than in most of Central Europe. Without the energy sector, the collapse could have been even worse, as it was in Ukraine. There were always good reasons to assume that the transition would be particularly difficult in Russia, but it is hard not to put some of the blame on the extreme liberalization program. A more carefully planned and implemented liberalization, with greater attention to macroeconomic stabilization, would have been less disruptive. The full liberalization of the trade sector and the collapse of the exchange rate led to the introduction of differential subsidies, often determined arbitrarily by officials who were under constant pressure from various interest groups. And the collapse of the ruble created a predictable need to impose taxes and other constraints on exports, followed in turn by a flood of differential exemptions issued discretionally at different levels of government.

A related lesson is that, given the opportunity, government officials at all levels will use their power to make discretionary decisions that will undercut one of the main objectives of reform: to formulate and enforce a set of clear, transparent, and uniform rules. This contradiction presents a serious policy dilemma.

In the not too distant future, the rate of exchange in Russia may recover to more normal levels, nearer the PPP rate. At that point some of the issues of excessive competition from imports may become more relevant. The potential for export earnings through the development of Russia's large internal market and abundant natural resources creates some options for trade policy that are not available to the smaller economies of Central Europe. At least in principle, Russia could devise a mixed strategy of industrial restructuring based on both export growth and import substitution.

Principles for an Optimal Russian Trade Policy

Like most other former Soviet republics, Russia would benefit greatly from expanded economic relations with the West. Those relations would be of two main types. The first would consist of activities geared to building a market economy and its institutions: such as the development and dissemination of a spirit of competition, the culture of market operation, modern management, and private enterprises of all kinds; assistance in the creation of the service sector, trade, finance, and business and private services; help in building the legal, regulatory, and enforcement mechanisms for market activities of all kinds, including the conduct of foreign trade; and assistance in expanding communication and information networks. The second category of foreign involvement would consist of the transfer of modern technology and capital equipment for the restructuring and upgrading of production in industry and other branches of the economy. The first cluster is the more important and urgent, and it will also facilitate action on the second.

The modes of involvement range from direct technical assistance and training, through all types of direct investment and joint ventures, to active trade. Russia is a very large country and economic restructuring is primarily a task for the Russians, but foreign involvement can play a critical role in some areas with large multiplier effects.

Outside participation, however, will depend on the course of the internal economic reforms. A stable and hospitable macroeconomic environment, a proper legal infrastructure (on property rights, business conduct, contract laws, and the like), political stability, and a long-term commitment to economic reform must all be created, so as to attract maximum outside participation and provide the best conditions for its dissemination. Thus far, Russia has not been able to create a stable commercial environment, and external private sector involvement has been limited.

Given the importance of foreign involvement to continued economic development, maximum openness seems vital, along with the free movement of goods, services, capital, and other factors and strong assurances of stable, predictable, and discretion-free treatment of foreign businesses. Regulations and rules, regarding both shallow and deep integration should be made as compatible as possible with established international accords, standards, and norms. These measures would also help the government resolve the difficulties that stand in the way of establishing effective foreign exchange and tariff regimes. The simpler and more uniform the laws and regulations and the lower the barriers, the greater the chances of effective enforcement, and the less the risk of arbitrariness and corruption.

However, full convertibility of the ruble and low tariff barriers for the movement of goods and services are not fully consistent with two other conditions in Russia: the macroeconomic instability and the time needed for the domestic industries to restructure.

It is widely believed that Russia will have great difficulty restoring macroeconomic stability with a freely fluctuating exchange rate. A fixed or pegged exchange rate, for at least a number of years, seems to offer greater hope of achieving successful stabilization.[25] As other countries faced with the need to restore stability have discovered, the internal use of foreign currencies for purposes other than long-term saving needs to be temporarily curtailed.[26] Furthermore, convertibility of the currency for capital account transactions, with its potential for currency speculation, can only be established after a considerable period of credible stabilization.[27]

The absence of full capital convertibility for the local population and entrepreneurs does not preclude the free movement of capital across borders by foreign investors. As is the case in many countries, foreign investors can enjoy special rights to take out profits and to withdraw their original investments. Their primary concern is the risk of a sharp devaluation and political changes that would reduce the value of their investments. Both of these risks are currently high in the case of Russia. Thus, clear and generous rules for the repatriation of foreign capital, supported by internationally financed insurance programs, are important preconditions for expanding the role of foreign direct investment.

There is an additional conflict in the area of trade. On the one hand, it is vital to open the economy up as much as possible, to facilitate rapid restructuring. On the other hand, it is important to gradually expose existing inefficient—though salvageable—enterprises and industries to external competition, to prevent their destruction in face of the much more efficient and superior world market products.

25. See Sachs (1994a); Fischer (1993); Bruno (1993, chaps. 7, 8); Aslund (1993); Ofer (1992). Included above are some who came to this conclusion rather late, and only after the regime of the free-exchange rate in Russia contributed to the development of the rapid inflation there during 1992. One wonders whether a program that would have a fixed exchange rate at the outset could not have reduced the rate of inflation, or even prevented it.

26. There is very little disagreement among economists regarding this point. See references in note 25, as well as in Blejer (1993).

27. van Brabant (1993a, 1993b).

As noted earlier, this threat looms large in Russia, where the export of energy and crudely processed raw materials can finance a large portion of imports. Despite the current low value of the ruble, a program that takes into account the long period of restructuring and anticipates success in the stabilization effort should incorporate full current account convertibility and a uniform exchange rate, but with the provision of a gradually declining level of protection for Russian industry. Such a scheme should involve no restrictions on exports, and the initial levels of protection should be sufficiently low to exert immediate pressure to act seriously on restructuring but should be high enough to prevent immediate closure.

Thus, there is justification for a temporary shield against imports in the need to preserve many of the former industries and part of the original enterprises—with their skilled labor, still usable equipment and structures, R&D facilities, and supply networks—as bases for restructuring. In order to survive, many of the enterprises will shed portions of their work forces and other facilities, thereby creating enough slack in the economy for new entrepreneurs to move in and provide these enterprises with the needed competition. Some will split up into smaller, more viable units, and others will close down. Many of the original enterprises are now being privatized and will, it is hoped, have the opportunity to install new managements and to bring in foreign partners and advisers. There is a good reason to believe that maintaining many of the enterprises as going concerns will limit and smooth the decline in production and expedite the transition.

Considering the length of the restructuring process, the majority of the Russian population will continue to consume, for a considerable period of time, only slightly improved versions of the low-quality products available in the past. Many enterprises will install only slightly improved domestic equipment and tools for that production. And the improvement in efficiency will be gradual and slow. Yet a premature closing of old plants, under intense pressures from foreign competitors, in order to clear the ground for new ones is much too expensive a move.

Nor is it feasible, from a social or political perspective, to eliminate many long-established enterprises. A country cannot abruptly shed a large proportion of its industrial base without unacceptable turmoil that may topple the entire reform effort. And there are not enough resources to support the population in the meantime. Politically, such a program is bound to fail in favor of a less optimal, highly protective regime that will hold on to inefficiencies much longer than necessary.

The protection accorded to Russian industry should be as low as possible, completely embodied in a simple tariff structure—without quotas—and transparent to all. There should also be a preannounced timetable for the gradual reductions of the tariffs. And, if at all possible, such a scheme should be incorporated into an international agreement: it could be part of the process of joining GATT, for example. Making the program of reduced protection part of an inter-national commitment to move toward freer trade would give it greater credibility and protection against internal pressures. Negotiations should be flexible with regard to the initial level of protection. A low tariff structure, for instance, may be simple but often results in more distortion and disguised protection. The somewhat softened bite of international competition, because of the proposed protective tariff, should be at least partly offset by the incentives created through such protection for potential foreign investors to move in to capture part of the large internal market.

Such a scheme of predetermined declining protection has not been common among other countries that have undertaken liberalization programs. In most cases, the liberalization was much less predeter-mined and consistent, and there were many retreats and complete failures.[28]

The automotive industry in Russia may serve as an illustration of the problems. It was a neglected area of domestic demand under the old regime. For many years, private transportation needs were di-rected to public means, so that the number of private automobiles per 1,000 people was just 56 in 1989, the lowest in Europe. In the 1960s a Fiat plant was imported and a number of models based on the old Fiat-124 are still being produced (the most famous is the Lada, which was exported to Central Europe and even to some countries in the West). Gasoline stations for private cars were almost nonexistent, and service garages were one of the most sought places of the second economy. With a shift to consumer sovereignty, the demand for pri-

---

28. Michaely, Papageorgiou, and Choksi (1991). It is true that the experiences of liberalization discussed in that study are real experiences rather than blueprints, but nevertheless they are indicative of feasible norms of opening up.

vate automobiles and related industries and services will eventually catch up with the rest of the world, and therefore the industry has the potential to become one of the fastest-growing sectors of the Russian economy.

The question is whether there should be an indigenous Russian car industry. At present, the quality of Russian cars is very low, and there is little doubt that the free importation of automobiles would overwhelm the domestic industry. However, considering the dynamic potential to become competitive in this industry, Russia does seem to have quite a few important advantages: a large domestic market and a huge army of highly skilled technical personnel, equipment, and other inputs, coming from adjacent military industries. Furthermore, no modern indigenous automobile industry in the world ever developed without the initial protection of the domestic market.

Protection should not be extended to the services sector, where Russia should be interested in attracting as many joint ventures and investments as it can get. These include banks, investment and financial institutions, information services, communications, and other business services. Foreign supply of these services has only minimal implication for reduced domestic employment, and international participation would provide an opportunity to develop these services from the beginning, in accord with international norms, facilitating deeper future integration. In exchange, Russia can demand equivalent treatment for its potential export of services based on highly skilled and relatively low-paid scientific, engineering, and technical personnel, in construction projects, in shipping, and in scientific services.

Trade and Reforms in Other Former Soviet States

Like Russia, the other fourteen newly created states inherited the socialist system described earlier, and in this sense face a similar set of transition problems. Yet each new state took with it a different slice of the Soviet apple, a somewhat distinct legacy of economic and trade relations, along with its own specific economic characteristics and its own bundle of political and historical problems. Add the differences in the general approach to reforms and in basic capabilities of the new governments, and the common systemic heritage may result in a wide range of different outcomes.

Upon the dissolution of the union, each new state faced an enormous set of problems requiring immediate action. Each had to confront the immediate consequences of the breakup, forge a transition strategy for the short and medium term, and begin to plan for its longer-term economic structure. To do so, they had to establish new governments with sharply changed responsibilities. While deciding on the nature of the internal reforms, they also had to develop new foreign economic policies, largely from scratch. Decisions had to be made about future economic and other relations with Russia and the other newly independent states. Suddenly, they were also free to conduct their own relations with the rest of the world, especially as they pertained to the global economy.

Main Features

One of the first republics to declare independence and to issue its own currency was Ukraine.[29] It is the second largest state of the former union, is Slavic like Russia, was part of the Russian empire long before the socialist revolution, and has a large Russian minority. Large portions of the population have strong ill feelings toward Russia that go far back in time. Recently, tension has developed over nuclear disarmament, dividing the Black Sea fleet, the fate of the Russian-populated Crimea, and the large Russian minority in the eastern provinces. The government of Ukraine had strong roots in the old Communist structures, and it has been quite nationalistic and conservative in its approach to economic reform. As a result, it has suffered one of the highest inflation rates and largest declines in output among the republics. Although the recently elected parliament (spring 1994) is not less conservative, the newly elected president, Leonid Kuchma, favors closer political and economic relations with Russia, and he is more disposed to undertake reform. In October 1994, following intensive discussion with the IMF, Kuchma announced a radical reform package, accompanied by an IMF loan, and this package was even approved by the parliament. Only time will tell whether this is a

29. Economic data on the former Soviet states before the disintegration of the Soviet Union are presented in table 3-1, and their performance under the early years following the dissolution in tables 3-2 and 3-3. The information on the individual states is based on De Melo, Denizer, and Gelb (forthcoming a); Kirmani, Enders, and Corsepius (1994); Plan-Econ (1994a); WEFA (1992); Radio Free Europe/Radio Liberty (1994).

new beginning for Ukraine. Although Ukraine has a significantly lower level of GNP per capita than Russia, its industrial structure is rather similar, especially in the emphasis on heavy industry. It is more agrarian than Russia and used to export food to Russia and the other republics. Most important, it lacks the energy resources of Russia. Because of the structure of its production, its present capability to export to Western markets is only limited. By the end of 1994 early signs of improvement were appearing.

Belarus, also Slavic and part of Russia for a long time, is similar to Russia in being overindustrialized, but it is even poorer in natural resources than Ukraine. Belarus was known as the assembly line of Russia: it used to produce and resell a wide range of producer and consumer goods and food products, based on inputs imported from the other Soviet republics. Of all the former republics, it depended on trade with the Soviet bloc the most. Like Ukraine, Belarus has had a conservative government and has undertaken few reforms. Unlike Ukraine, however, it declared independence halfheartedly and always sought to preserve close economic ties with Russia and the other states. It thus moved cautiously to undertake a reform program. At the beginning, that translated into the smallest output decline, but very little reform. Mere delaying of the reforms, however, did not work, and in 1993 Belarus fell into the common syndrome of high inflation and a steep decline in output. The newly elected president (July 1994) seems to favor still closer ties, even virtual reunification, and a continuation of a timid and populist approach to economic reform.

Also in the West is Moldova, a small, highly agrarian state that is the least industrialized among the European states. It was annexed to the Soviet Union from Romania in 1940. Since its independence it has been involved in an internal conflict with a self-declared Dniester republic dominated by a militant Russian minority. After initially flirting with the idea of reunification with Romania, the government now seems to favor closer cooperation with Russia. Moldova has followed Russia in its reform program, and in this respect it is much more advanced than its immediate neighbors.

Next are the three small Baltic states, which were incorporated into the Soviet Union by force in 1939: Estonia, Latvia, and Lithuania. They have strong cultural and historical links with the Nordic states, Germany, and Poland. Each has large Russian minorities, however.

Between the two world wars they had some experience with a rudimentary market economy and industrialization, but they were part of the Russian empire before World War I. Estonia and Latvia were the most developed republics in the union, and all three had large manufacturing sectors and highly qualified labor forces. A significant part of their manufacturing activity was in consumer goods and processed food, so restructuring may be somewhat less difficult for them. The Russian minorities, however, were typically employed in military production and other heavy industry.

The Baltic states were the first to separate from the Soviet Union and declare independence. All considered themselves under Soviet occupation since 1940 and view the large Russian minorities as a constant threat. All three (Lithuania to a lesser extent) embarked on a course of radical reforms, including opening up toward the global market; and all paid dearly in lost output, falling standards of living, and inflation. More recently, they have succeeded in reducing the rate of inflation, reversing the initial decline in output, and reorienting their economies away from the other republics and toward the West.[30]

There are six Muslim states: Azerbaijan in the Caucasus, and the others in Central Asia. Among them, Kazakhstan has a large Russian minority, and it is the most economically developed of the group. These six states, together with the two small ethnic Christian states in the Caucasus, Armenia and Georgia, make up the least-developed states of the union. With the exception of Armenia, they are highly agrarian, with a low degree of industrialization, even by nonsocialist standards.[31] Kazakhstan and Uzbekistan are of medium size in terms of population, but all the other states in the group are small. Among the Muslim states, Turkmenistan, Azerbaijan, and Kazakhstan have abundant natural resources, but the others also have some.

One of the main problems for most of these states may prove to be political. Several have found themselves engaged in military conflicts. These have been internal disputes in Georgia and Tajikistan and involved neighboring states in Azerbaijan and Armenia. So far, these conflicts have absorbed their main energies, at the cost of their reform programs. Georgia and Armenia did take a number of important

---

30. See also IMF (1993b, 1993c, 1993d). In 1993, Lithuania elected a more conservative government that slowed the pace of the reforms to some extent.
31. Easterly and Fischer (1993).

reform steps, and in some respects they are more advanced than Russia. Armenia, for example, has already privatized agriculture. However, they have not benefited from their reforms because of the conflicts.

From an economic perspective, the six Muslim states should require less restructuring of production because of their lower degree of industrialization, and their manufacturing sectors are more "normally" concentrated in consumer, light manufacturing, and food industries. In this respect, their situation resembles that of China. Those among them with a rich endowment of natural resources—Turkmenistan, Azerbaijan, Kazakhstan—can finance a portion of the industrialization through their own means, and they should be able to attract foreign investment. Four of the more peaceful states in Central Asia—Kyrgyz Republic, Turkmenistan, Uzbekistan, and Azerbaijan—are still governed by the old structures, although they all went through so-called democratic elections and are moving very cautiously on economic reform.[32] Kazakhstan, like Russia, has undertaken bolder reform steps, but they have been incomplete in critical respects.[33] Kazakhstan is also the only Muslim state with a sizable Russian minority, a large resource base, and a heavy manufacturing sector, which make it more similar to Russia.

Interrepublic Trade and Cooperation

During the Soviet period, all fifteen republics were integrated into one economy and one planning system, with a high level of interdependence, under the hegemony and dominance of the central government, in most respects meaning Russia. The planning authority treated the union as one country, but the government also used its political power to determine the direction of development and the patterns of specialization among the republics, with one objective being to ensure Russian dominance. The structure of trade resembled a hub-and-spoke system with Russia at the center. Russia also dominated trade with regions outside the union. Trade between the repub-

32. Kyrgystan and Azerbaijan are somewhat more dynamic with respect to reforms. The latter initiated radical reform early in 1994, including privatization and liberalization of the trade regime. See Connolly and Vatnick (1994); De Melo, Denizer, and Gelb (forthcoming a).

33. Fischer (1993); Kirmani, Enders, and Corsepius (1994); Michalopoulos and Tarr (1994).

Table 3-8. *Russian Trade with the Other Republics of the Former Soviet Union, by Commodity Group, 1990*
Percent of total

	Domestic prices			Net exports, world market prices
Commodity group	Exports	Imports	Net exports	
Industry	95.7	94.8	104.3	100.4
Energy	13.0	4.4	91.0	76.9
Ferrous metals	7.8	8.8	−1.1	−0.3
Nonferrous metals	4.4	2.4	22.8	9.0
Chemicals	12.2	8.3	47.9	24.4
Timber and construction materials	6.5	2.2	44.9	7.2
Machine building	34.9	30.8	72.3	16.5
Light and food industry	13.3	35.7	−189.8	−25.2
Other industry	3.5	2.1	16.2	3.5
Agriculture	1.2	4.0	−24.7	−2.4
Other	3.1	1.2	20.4	1.9
Total, billions of rubles	74.7	67.3	7.4	31.2

Source: Christensen (1994, table A3).

lics was composed of a high share of each republic's output, between 40 percent and 70 percent of NMP, and only Kazakhstan had a low trade ratio (table 3-4). Many of the republics depended on Russia for their energy supplies and in return provided products of light industry and agriculture (table 3-8).[34]

In addition to these traded goods, there was a significant net flow of resources from the center (Russia) to the republics. These subsidies went through two main channels: distorted relative prices, mostly in the form of low energy prices, and direct budgetary transfers. As can be seen from table 3-4, the trade subsidy alone amounted to 8 percent of Russian NMP just before the dissolution of the union, and up to a third, even 40 percent, of the NMP of some republics.

The formal dissolution of the union at the end of 1991 and the liberalization of prices in Russia caused a major disruption of this interstate trade. Indeed, trade between the former republics (and other regions) was already disrupted to some extent during 1991 as

34. The trade of each republic for seven commodity groups is summarized in appendix table 3-A2.

the republics tried to secure goods in short supply for their residents, and some were also engaged in an early struggle for independence. In view of the lack of preparation for the dissolution, it is not surprising that the volume of interstate trade collapsed to half its original level during 1992 and fed into a downward spiral of production.

To begin with, the dissolution turned a large volume of what had been internal trade into interstate trade that needed, but lacked, a new institutional infrastructure. In addition, the radical changes in relative prices completely altered the established terms of trade among the republics, introduced confusion, and created pressures for political intervention to protect existing interests. Also, immediate questions arose about the continuation of Russian aid. Since much of the aid was embodied in low energy prices, and since these prices were about to increase sharply, the continuation of concessionary energy prices (and those of a few other basic materials) became a major issue in the decision on the future of economic relations between individual states and Russia. Maintaining the ruble zone was seen as a way of preserving high levels of Russian support to the other republics, perhaps as much as 10 percent of GNP.[35]

Despite the political dissolution of the Soviet Union, it continued to exist for a long time in the form of a de facto monetary union, based on the ruble. All the newly established states stayed, almost by default, within the ruble area. They benefited together from the liberalization and suffered together from the inflationary pressures and the monetary overhang that developed before 1992. They were caught unprepared and had little choice but to accept the price changes and the open inflation that followed. The chaotic macroeconomic environment that emerged put additional strains on the trade between them.

Part of the former intra-Soviet trade (and the relevant output) should have been eliminated because it was geared to an outdated

35. According to Tepluxin and Normaka (1994), Russian net subsidies to other states of the union amounted in 1992 to between $8.4 and $24.5 billion. The latter is the total amount resulting from differences between world market prices and prices actually charged. The former includes only subsidies for Russian goods that were actually sold on the world market. Energy prices to the states were between 10 and 30 percent of world market prices, a difference that embodied most of the subsidy. In many cases, export prices to the states were lower than in Russia. The main debtors among them in 1992 were Ukraine, Kazakhstan, and Uzbekistan. For further discussion see Sachs (1994b); Konovalov (1994).

basket of goods, such as military production, or because it was based on highly distorted prices and thus the wrong comparative advantage. Ideally, new channels of trade, payment principles, and institutions would clearly discriminate against "old and bad" deals and would preserve only "new and good" ones. The needed network was not created, however, and many good deals were thrown away with the bad. Another part of the old trade should have been maintained during a transition period until new, more efficient sources of supply could be developed. In practice, decisions were driven by other factors, such as Russia's desire to reduce the subsidies it provided other states, the long-standing national animosities, and the desire of the other states to continue receiving low-cost energy. The dilemma Russia faces is how to be a political and strategic leader of the "near abroad" and yet not pay too much for that status.

The spread of price liberalization across the entire region in early 1992 and the decision to keep the ruble as a common currency were intended in the first place to keep trade moving across the new borders. Efforts to maintain different price structures or to immediately introduce separate currencies would have probably increased the initial confusion. Furthermore, the creation of some transitional payments union was probably no more possible than in the case of the CMEA.

This policy was plagued with two major problems. First, the governments of all the new states were ill prepared and lacked the capability and political leadership to manage such a radical change. Many states attempted to prevent price changes for key products and to stop the inflation by continuing partial price controls and heavy subsidies. These acts necessitated strict restrictions on exports of goods with controlled prices, restrictions that produced retaliation and a further shrinkage of trade. Second, the ruble area lacked a central unified monetary authority. Rather, the central banks of all the new states could continue to create ruble credits (printing of cash Russian rubles remained in the hands of the Central Bank of Russia) to finance government deficits, domestic production needs, and imports from Russia.[36] These credits fueled inflation in the entire

---

36. In 1992 between 25 and 30 percent of all the ruble notes printed in Russia were sent to other states. This consisted of about one-quarter of the total Russian credits granted to them. See Tepluxin and Normaka (1994).

zone, but also helped to perpetuate unwanted surplus Russian trade balances: that is, the old aid flows to the other republics. In effect, it was a monetary system with multiple central banks.

Thus there was a long delay in creating new payment mechanisms to facilitate "good" trade. Such new mechanisms, mostly through new banks, have improved in recent months. However, bilateral trade agreements between governments, with obligatory deliveries and the involvement of state trading organizations, as well as barter deals, still account for a high proportion of the trade. In a way, the hesitation to create new instruments brought the old ones back, and it is not clear whether the new composition of trade has shifted (on a net basis) in the right direction.

THE END OF MONETARY UNION. Beginning in the middle of 1992, Russia acted to protect itself against the importation of higher inflation from the periphery, and to control its subsidization of the other states. The most important action was to limit the issuance of ruble credits by other central banks to finance imports from Russia. Special correspondence accounts, with credit limits, were established among the central banks. The resulting shortage of rubles in all other states prompted them to issue various types of nonconvertible parallel currencies (coupons and the like). These new currencies suffered from even higher inflation than in Russia and depreciated, sometimes severely, against the ruble. Yet as long as they remained nonconvertible, the ruble continued as the main medium of trade. Russia also made clear that the supply of cheap energy and the granting of Russian credits and aid would be drastically reduced and phased out. Net assistance to the republics by Russia was reduced significantly. It declined in 1993 to about half the 1992 level, although Russia still had a big trade surplus with the other republics. The imbalance was almost eliminated in 1994, but Russia faces great difficulties in collecting old debts.[37]

With these actions, Russia imposed tough conditions on any state that wanted to stay in the ruble zone, requiring it to give up an independent monetary policy, to walk in tandem with Russia in fiscal policy and economic reform, and to accept a variety of Russian controls. By the end of 1993 such harsh conditions were

37. Konovalov (1994); Tepluxin and Normaka (1994).

only accepted by Tajikistan.[38] The others left the ruble zone.[39] In most cases, the new currencies are allowed to fluctuate in relation to the ruble.

THE NEW TRADE SYSTEM. The evolution of a new payments system coincided with the development of new trade policies. The initial sharp fall in trade volume, the deficits of the other states in trade with Russia, and the bad experience with the attempt to base CMEA trade on hard currencies forced Russia and its partners to once again rely on bilateral intergovernment trade agreements. These new agreements started in March 1992, and typically developed "obligatory," "indicative," and free lists of traded goods. Goods on the first two lists specified the quantities to be traded. Many of the obligatory deals also included maximum prices, although enterprises were allowed to negotiate prices for goods on the indicative list. On top of these two lists, free trade was allowed through the correspondent accounts discussed above.

This three-tier arrangement prevented a total collapse of trade, provided a means of maintaining prices at levels different from those in the world markets (such as energy prices), and ensured a supply of essential inputs, thus keeping production going. The system also provided the flexibility needed to deal with states that had differing levels of economic reform and different trade regimes. It also embodied built-in dynamics that made it possible to shift the proportions of trade among the three levels and gradually move toward freer trade. Over time, the proportions of traded goods on the free list tended to expand, but bilateral deals reemerged whenever trade difficulties arose. The disadvantage of the bilateral agreements is that they reduce the pressure to reform, maintain unwarranted trade (and production), and leave too much to bureaucratic discretion (and corruption). The system is still the main means of trade for those states with slow-moving reforms, notably Belarus.

---

38. Belarus and Russia have been negotiating a monetary union and trade agreement over the past year, but, by the summer of 1994, the agreement over the monetary union was still to be signed. Interestingly, this agreement faced stronger opposition in Russia than in Belarus. For details see Whitlock (1994); Markus (1994); Kirmani, Enders, and Corsepius (1994); Christensen (1994).

39. The Baltic states were among the first to abandon the ruble and establish their own convertible currency. Since they also liberalized prices, the rate of inflation in 1992 was similar to that of the other states; but it was reduced to moderate rates during 1993.

Even with the trade agreements, there was substantial uncertainty about timing and other clearing mechanisms, compliance enforcement, and dispute settlement; and even the obligatory agreements were only partly fulfilled. Many of the governments have had trouble imposing their will on the enterprises. Trade among the states was also used as a means of illegally exporting raw materials to the West. With border and customs stations still being established, there was limited control and many gaps in recording. Almost all the agreements, including the clearing arrangements, were bilateral. This left little room for multilateral deals.

During 1992 most interstate trade was free of tariffs, although in many cases traders had to comply with other types of trade restrictions (such as quotas, the surrender of part of the hard currency proceeds, and licensing). Toward the end of 1992 and during 1993 the individual states began to introduce their own tariff systems. In 1993, for example, Russia collected export taxes on relevant goods belonging to the nonobligatory lists, demanded export licenses for all exports not on the free list, and imposed import tariffs on some goods belonging to the lower lists.[40] At the same time, a number of free-trade (no-tariff) or MFN (preferential tariffs) agreements were concluded among some former Soviet states. Under both arrangements, there were still export taxes, various quotas, the need for export licensing, and other barriers. For example, a free-trade agreement was signed among the three Baltic states in September 1993, and they have signed MFN agreements with some of the other states.

OTHER AREAS OF COOPERATION. The republics have discussed other forms of economic cooperation, but have done little to implement them. Negotiations have been taking place to form a Slavic economic union of Russia, Ukraine, Belarus, and Kazakhstan. Similarly, there has been some talk of forming a Central Asian common market, and there is a loose organization of all Central Asian countries, including Afghanistan, Iran, and Turkey. Negotiations have also been held to consider a CIS economic union under which there might be free flows of goods, labor, and capital among the members, as well as multilateral payment arrangements, and an outside common tariff.

---

40. Tepluxin and Normaka (1994); Konovalov (1994); Kirmani, Enders, and Corsepius (1994).

Various agreements of this kind were signed in principle (including similar agreements with only a number of states), but up to this point no concrete action has been taken.

The tone of these discussions changed somewhat in 1993. Previously, Russia had sought to keep the union together, whereas most of the other states were intent on gaining their independence in every respect. During 1993 the other states began recognizing the economic benefits of closer cooperation with Russia. Meanwhile, Russia, while still interested politically, began to impose tougher economic conditions. In the two recent elections in Belarus and in Ukraine, the candidates who emphasized cooperation with Russia were elected. Another source of tension between Russia and the periphery is Russia's desire to keep trade moving in a bilateral, Russia-centered fashion, as in the old days. The other states would like to use the various CIS instruments to establish multilateral trade and other economic relations.

Trade Outside the Former Soviet Union

At the same time that these new trade arrangements were being reshaped, the republics all tried to reach trade agreements with countries outside the former Soviet Union. During 1992 a number of old-fashioned bilateral trade agreements were signed, especially with former CMEA or socialist countries, as well as a number of developing countries. Some of these agreements were phased out later as more Western-style trade relations were established.

All the former Soviet countries tried to gain, and most succeeded, some status with GATT, the IMF, and the World Bank, as well as preferential trade agreements with Western countries, especially the United States and the European Union. The Baltic countries also secured a number of free-trade accords with the Scandinavian countries. Despite these agreements, countries of the West still maintain substantial discriminatory tariffs as well as nontariff barriers on many primary and other products from the states of the former Soviet bloc.[41]

41. Kirmani, Enders, and Corsepius (1994).

The evolution of the trade regimes in the various republics was similar in principle to that in Russia, but varied according to the pace of economic reform and the level of stabilization. Most states have eliminated the government monopoly over trade and have reduced the portion of trade conducted by government organizations. Government intervention remains substantial, however, in those states that are taking longer to introduce general economic reforms, such as Ukraine, Belarus, and some of the Central Asian republics. Initially the state trade monopoly was replaced by a battery of other regulations, including foreign exchange surrender requirements (sometimes at highly concessionary rates), export quotas, export licensing, and import subsidies and licensing. Recently, there has been a gradual trend toward removing these restrictions in favor of taxes on exports and imports, and toward making the tariff structure more uniform. Some states have also moved to unify the exchange rate system and to introduce current account convertibility. When rates of exchange began to appreciate, import subsidies were gradually abolished and replaced with low and uniform tariffs, in the range of 5–25 percent, but these are now growing. In addition, export restrictions were gradually unified and even eliminated.[42]

Throughout the initial period of transition, the extremely undervalued domestic currencies provided a shield against imports from the outside and created an artificial trade zone among most of the states. Internally, however, varying degrees of undervaluation, as well as different levels of price controls, created large opportunities for arbitrage across borders. States protected themselves against such pressures by keeping their domestic currencies nonconvertible and imposing other export restrictions. As this artificial shield gradually declines, at different rates in the individual states, pressures for protection of domestic production will increase, and each state will have to determine its trade policy toward the others and toward the rest of the world. Such pressures have already been mounting in the Baltic states, and in Russia, where some degree of success in stabilization significantly raised the value of the domestic currency. In a few cases, high import tariffs as well as quantitative restrictions have already been imposed, especially in the sphere of agriculture.

---

42. A detailed account of these trends through the end of 1993 can be found in Kirmani, Enders, and Corsepius (1994).

All the above changes, in addition to the major political and other economic reforms, were bound to affect the volume and composition of trade among the former Soviet states. Although some new trade has developed with the West, the economic decline and the extreme shortage of hard currency have sharply limited affordable imports. In some cases, revenues from exports to the West must be used to pay higher bills for energy purchases from Russia (Ukraine, Belarus). The new exports outside the region consist of primary goods, energy, metals (aluminum), and some agricultural products. Except for energy, the ability to export those products depends on the extreme undervaluation of the local currencies. Because most of the observed changes in trade flows are the result of the disruption of trade within the zone and the extreme undervaluation of exchange rates, they cannot be said to indicate the new pattern of trade that will emerge under more normal conditions in the future.

Policy Considerations

What points should these states be considering in their search for an appropriate trade policy? First, a high level of interstate trade offers significant advantages that extend to Russia as well as the other states. In the short run, trade within the old supply network would reduce some of the disruption of the economic transition. Over the longer term, some of the complementarity created during the long years of membership in an economic union may have the potential to develop into a lasting comparative advantage. Thus efforts to revive interstate trade should be accorded a high priority. In practice, however, most of that trade was between each republic and Russia, not among the peripheral states. Russia plays the central role in any such decision, and a trade association that excludes Russia has limited value.

The advantages of intensive interstate trade seem greatest for the more industrially and economically advanced states to the north and west of Russia, namely, the Baltics and Belarus. They may be able to secure a market for some of their consumer manufactures, upper-level producer goods, and processed food, in exchange for supplies of energy and other raw materials. There are also benefits to the less-developed states in the Caucasus and Central Asia, whose potential exports consist of primary goods, agriculture, and light manufactures. These products face low demand and trade barriers in the West.

Many of these states have traditionally relied on Russia to handle their exports, and they are unprepared institutionally to engage in international trade. Others are isolated geographically from the global markets. The benefits are least for some of the resource-rich states such as Turkmenistan (gas), Azerbaijan (oil), Uzbekistan (gold). They have alternative trade routes through states that neighbor the old Soviet Union. Also, those states with a low degree of industrialization and significant natural resources will be more able to break with the old production relationships and obtain foreign partners.

Earlier we suggested that a temporary protective tariff for Russian manufacturing might be justified to provide time for restructuring. No such rationale exists for tariffs between Russia and the other states of the old union, whose industries are equally in need of restructuring. Thus free-trade agreements between Russia and the other states would be one positive form of increased cooperation.

In all cases, however, the extent of trade cooperation will depend on whether the states, especially Russia, manage to stabilize their economies and turn around the decline in production. Such cooperation will also depend on Russia's willingness to provide economic support to some of the other states. If the recent economic trends in Russia—declining rates of inflation, stabilization of production, and continued privatization—can be sustained, economic cooperation with Russia could assist the transition across the entire region. Indeed, Russia may regain the role of a leader in promoting change. At the same time, advocating greater cooperation in the region does not mean retreating from economic reform, behind the shield of a new socialist region. To the maximum feasible extent, more stable trade relations within the region should be based on market principles.

Even more than Russia, each of the other states must open up to the world market in terms of trade and investment: they are too small to rely on internal markets, and they need all forms of foreign assistance. They have more to gain from opening up and more to lose from isolation. An open trade policy with the rest of the world is also an important counterweight to offset any tendency to maintain the distortions and inefficiencies embodied in the present trade within the zone. Some smaller states also have the potential to establish more cohesive programs that have a better chance of attracting international involvement.

The Baltic republics, with Estonia as a pioneer, started early in 1992 to redirect their economies toward the West, although at a heavy cost of declining production and sharply higher prices for Russian energy and other inputs. The subsidies embodied in their trade imbalance with Russia during the Soviet period were among the highest in the union, as can be observed from the very high ratios of trade deficits with Russia estimated at world market prices (table 3-4). There are strong political and national motivations for the change, but also an economic rationale. Their small size and location, the potential close relations with the Nordic countries, prior experience with a market economy up to 1939, and the relatively high level of economic development and labor force skills should all help facilitate restructuring through a reorientation toward the West. The transition may be somewhat easier for Estonia and less so for Lithuania, which is poorer and less industrialized.

Yet these countries would still gain from continued trade relations with Russia, whether within a regional framework or not. They all have several major enterprises with close supply connections with enterprises in Russia (many employ Russian nationals), and a coordinated restructuring could be helpful. Prior trade networks suggest advantages in the purchase of raw materials, and in the supply to Russia of processed agricultural products, mostly in the meat and dairy sectors.

These countries—because of their growing relations with the West on the one hand and their deep knowledge of the old union and prior experience in doing business with Russia and the other states on the other—have the potential to serve as a commercial and technological bridge between the West and the region. They might assist in the marketing of Russian exports to the global economy, and in channeling Western technologies and products into Russia and the other former Soviet states.

Belarus is the most extreme case of historical integration with the Russian economy because of its well-educated work force and its lack of significant natural resources. It was one of the few republics with a surplus balance of trade with Russia under the old regime, and, among the energy-poor republics, the one with the lowest embodied subsidies (table 3-4). In some respects Belarus is similar to the Baltic states and the Central European countries, although it is larger than the Baltic states and much more dependent on Russia. By balancing both relationships—opening up to the West, but continuing to trade with Russia (inside a free-trade zone)—it also may be able to position itself as an economic bridge between the West and the East.

Ukraine faces many of the same reform issues as Russia, with one major difference: it lacks a significant source of energy. Like Russia, it has concentrated production in heavy industry, metalworking, and heavy machinery, but has a trade deficit in consumer goods (other than food). Under these circumstances, it will have great difficulties in reorienting itself toward the West and has few potential resources that may be used to generate hard currencies in the short term. The lack of obvious export potential in the short run will force Ukraine to keep a rather low hard currency wage for some time and to restructure under strong world market pressure.

Conclusion

All the states of the former Soviet Union carry a heavy heritage of a long functional isolation from the world markets, a distorted structure of production and prices, backward technology, and a large shortfall in the institutional infrastructure, tradition, and culture of a market economy. Many of the new states are highly industrialized, but in a way that is much different than the pattern in most market economies. All of this makes the economic transition and integration into the world economy very difficult and painful. At the same time, the extent of distortions also makes the payoff from a successful transition even more rewarding. The existence of large industrial sectors, the accompanying institutional and technological infrastructure, and high levels of skills and education among the population would seem to preclude a policy of "starting from scratch." Yet, the inability to manage the transition to date suggests that this is what may be happening.

Under central planning, the government played a role that was quite different from the one it is being called on to perform during the transition and beyond. It should be smaller and should change its emphasis from making decisions on resource allocation to setting and enforcing the rules by which private agents will operate. It needs to create a stable macroeconomic environment and calm political atmosphere in which private activity, both domestic and foreign, can flourish. This restructuring of government may be as difficult to carry out as the restructuring of the economy. The transition to markets involves a radical diminution of the role of government and a change in its mode of operation, but not its withering away. Yet it is extremely difficult to supplant an old government with a new one or to change the way of thinking of the existing bureaucracy. It follows that the transition should be based on the actions of private agents, while the government strives to make the environment for their action as friendly as possible.

This is especially true if these countries hope to attract foreign capital and entrepreneurship. Such capital is usually joined with know-how, technology, and international marketing networks. But foreign investment is drawn to countries with a stable and friendly commercial environment. Many of the states of the region have enormous economic potential, but most still lack the conditions for attracting foreign involvement.

The economic situation of most of these states calls for a mixed strategy toward reform. Restructuring certainly needs to be promoted by an internal policy of liberalization and conversion to markets and an external strategy of opening the economy to outside market forces. But a prudent and disciplined policy is also needed to preserve existing assets and provide the enterprises with the resources and time required to adjust to the new circumstances. As already pointed out, this process would be greatly assisted by strong efforts to restore interstate trade (and internal trade within Russia). But the new governments are all very weak, and calls for cooperation may make them fear they will lose their newly gained independence.

We believe that the development of a competitive manufacturing sector in these states will require a substantial period of low factor (wage) costs. For the time being, such costs are being provided by the severely depreciated value of their exchange rates, and thus low dollar wages. However, a successful stabilization program is likely to cause their exchange rates to return to more normal equilibrium values. There is a particular risk for Russia that its strong export potential from natural resources will result in an exchange rate above the level consistent with expansion of the domestic manufacturing base. This suggests the use of a temporary tariff surcharge on imports of manufactures. The surcharge could be combined with a free-trade agreement with the other states of the former Soviet Union to foster the development of a large internal market. The states should also move as rapidly as possible to establish current account convertibility with the global economy, with generous provisions for foreign direct investment. This would still leave them more open than many middle-income countries and some developed economies.

The short-term difficulties of achieving shallow integration with the global economy need not inhibit efforts to move ahead with some aspects of deep integration. These countries have a large comparative disadvantage in many market services, and the existing amount of resources devoted to such activities is small. They have the opportunity to import the latest technologies in these areas with little loss of existing assets. They can also introduce the last word in labor and social, antitrust, and other legislation so as to align themselves with the sought-after global uniformity in these areas.

Table 3-A1. *International and Interrepublic Trade, All States of the Former Soviet Union, 1990–93*
Millions of current dollars

Republic	1990 Exports	1990 Imports	1991 Exports	1991 Imports	1992 Exports	1992 Imports	1993 Exports	1993 Imports
International trade								
Russia	80,900	82,900	53,100	45,100	41,600	37,200	43,900	33,100
Ukraine	13,390	15,907	8,500	11,300	6,000	5,500	6,300	4,700
Kazakhstan	1,777	3,250	1,183	2,546	1,489	961	1,529	1,269
Belarus	3,438	5,256	1,661	1,957	1,061	755	737	777
Uzbekistan	1,390	2,217	1,257	2,048	869	929	1,466	1,280
Azerbaijan	723	1,413	487	1,248	754	333	351	241
Georgia	515	1,543	30	480	161	269	222	460
Lithuania	679	1,543	345	475	557	342	696	486
Moldova	405	1,432	180	656	157	170	174	210
Latvia	304	1,642	125	478	429	423	460	339
Armenia	109	855	70	830	40	95	29	188
Kyrgyz Republic	89	1,298	23	785	77	71	112	112
Tajikistan	609	655	424	706	111	132	263	374
Turkmenistan	195	523	146	618	1,145	543	1,156	749
Estonia	198	592	50	204	242	254	461	618

Interrepublic trade (at implicit exchange rates)

Russia	146,183	95,802	115,355	61,227	83,753	53,113	55,355	34,109
Ukraine	60,348	71,841	43,147	60,872	28,133	48,573	17,628	35,294
Kazakhstan	13,993	24,810	12,008	15,874	11,574	17,586	7,863	11,788
Belarus	27,660	28,740	19,977	21,640	15,636	16,568	12,144	13,739
Uzbekistan	11,327	18,818	9,228	11,715	4,177	5,818	4,100	5,243
Azerbaijan	8,213	7,300	6,167	6,347	3,144	2,972	1,555	1,526
Georgia	5,168	7,608	2,463	3,900	602	1,473	573	1,321
Lithuania	7,213	12,082	5,211	6,365	2,529	4,551	1,548	1,852
Moldova	4,984	8,442	2,552	5,019	1,337	3,093	1,203	2,417
Latvia	6,516	8,302	4,046	4,197	3,239	3,396	978	1,082
Armenia	3,509	5,477	1,882	3,766	1,335	1,339	583	999
Kyrgyz Republic	3,250	5,120	3,470	3,628	1,599	2,048	814	1,175
Tajikistan	2,760	5,375	1,886	3,662	495	1,186	292	611
Turkmenistan	4,603	4,042	4,883	2,646	4,691	3,055	2,734	2,717
Estonia	3,289	5,257	2,574	3,013	983	1,173	568	543

Source: Michalopoulos and Tarr (1994, tables 1.1 and 1.2).

Table 3-A2. *Trade Balance in Interrepublic and External Trade, Actual Trade Prices, 1989–90*

Commodity	Russia	Ukraine	Belarus	Estonia	Kazakhstan	Azerbaijan	Uzbekistan	Latvia	Lithuania	Moldova	Tajikistan	Turkmenistan	Armenia	Georgia	Kyrgyzstan
Interrepublic (domestic prices)															
Energy	+	–	–	–	–	+	–	–	–	–	–	+	–	–	–
Chemicals	+	+	+	–	–	+	–	–	–	–	–	–	+	–	–
Metals	+	+	–	–	+	–	–	–	–	–	=	–	–	–	–
Machinery	+	+	+	–	–	–	–	–	–	–	–	–	–	–	–
Light industry	–	–	+	+	–	+	+	+	+	+	+	+	+	+	+
Food industry	–	+	+	+	–	+	–	+	+	+	–	–	+	+	+
Agriculture	–	+	–	–	+	+	+	–	+	+	–	+	–	+	+
External															
Energy	+	+	–	–	+	+	+	–	+	+	–	–	–	+	–
Chemicals	+	–	+	–	...	–	–	–	–	–	–	–	–	–	–
Metals	...	+	+	–	+	–	–	=	–	–	–	–	–	+	–
Machinery	–	–	+	–	+	–	–	–	–	–	–	–	–	–	–
Light industry	–	–	+	+	–	–	–	=	–	–	–	–	–	–	–
Food industry	–	–	–	+	–	–	–	–	–	–	–	–	–	–	–
Agriculture	–	–	–	–	–	–	–	–	–	–	–	–	–	–	–

Source: World Bank (1993c).
Note: Surplus (+), deficit (–), or balance (=).

Chapter 4

Central Europe

SINCE 1990 the countries of Central Europe, excluding the former Yugoslavia, have taken large strides toward creating private market-based economies. They have managed to sustain democracy and avoid serious social unrest despite substantial economic dislocation and uncertainty. And, although they differ somewhat in the sequence and pace of reform, they are remarkably unanimous in their view of the ultimate goal and the basic elements of the transition. The reforms have been particularly rapid and far reaching with respect to foreign economic relations: they were designed to bring these countries closer to full integration into the global economy and membership in the European Union.

These countries are now beginning to diverge in more significant ways. The three large economies of Poland, Hungary, and the Czech Republic have reached the bottom of their economic decline and are experiencing a recovery of economic activity, albeit at modest rates. They have established a reasonable degree of macroeconomic stability, liberalized domestic prices, and opened their economies to global trade. They are moving into a second stage of privatizing their state enterprises, establishing a functioning financial system, and reforming their fiscal systems. Within the next two years, they will have completed much of the reform agenda laid out at the beginning of the decade. Their policies will then need to turn from reform to promoting economic growth. Slovenia and Slovakia are two smaller economies that also might be classified as having successfully completed many of the basic reforms. The rest of the countries in the region, however, are lagging behind, as many continue to experience declin-

Table 4-1. *Central Europe, Initial Conditions*

Indicator	Hungary	Poland	Czechoslovakia	Bulgaria	Romania
Population in mid-1989 (in millions)	10.6	37.9	15.6	9.0	23.2
GNP per capita in 1989 (US$ at PPP)	6,170	5,040	8,010	6,090	3,570
Administered prices (% of total)[a]	15	100[b]	100	100	80
State ownership (%)	90	70	95	95	85
General government balance in 1989 (% of GDP)	−1.3	−7.4	−2.4	−1.4	8.4
External debt, 1990 (% of GDP)	65.6	82.4	18.6	56.9	1.1
Current account, 1989 (% of GDP)	−4.9	−2.7	1.9	−5.9	13.1
Exports to CMEA, 1990					
Percent of total	43	41[c]	60	69	50
Percent of GDP	16	14	25	34	6

Sources: Bruno (1992, table 1); World Bank (1993d); OECD (1993a).
a. Status in late 1980s.
b. Excluding food prices.
c. 1989.

ing levels of output and serious economic instability. It is evident that all of them will take decades to catch up with Western Europe.

In several countries of Central Europe the reform process was initiated in an environment of macroeconomic imbalances. For the most part, they are industrial rather than agricultural economies and thus had numerous structural adjustment problems; yet the pace of reform has been fast and hectic. Reform has been accompanied by severe recession, rather than providing the stimulus to growth evident, say, in China. At the same time, they faced more favorable conditions than did the countries of the former Soviet Union. The largest of the Central European group had begun creating some of the institutions of a market economy in the 1980s; and, although the collapse of CMEA trade was a major shock to these economies, it was less disruptive than the breakup of the internal monetary and trade network of the Soviet Union. Except for Yugoslavia, they were also able to quickly establish stable political regimes, committed to economic reform. Some basic economic measures of the initial situations in six of these countries are provided in table 4-1. We have focused our attention on the three largest economies—the former Czechoslovakia,

Table 4-2. *Rate of Change of GDP, Selected Central European Economies,*
1990–94

Economy	1990	1991	1992	Cumulative, 1990–92	1993	Projected, 1994
Bulgaria	−9.1	−11.7	−5.7	−24.3	−4.2	−2.0
Czechoslovakia	−0.4	−15.9	−8.5	−23.4	. . .	. . .
Czech Republic	. . .	. . .	. . .	. . .	−0.3	1.5
Slovak Republic	. . .	. . .	. . .	. . .	−4.1	0.0
Hungary	−3.5	−9.9	−5.1	−17.5	−2.0	1.0
Poland	−11.6	−7.6	1.5	−17.5	4.0	4.5
Romania	−7.4	−15.1	−13.5	−32.0	1.0	0.0

Source: IMF (1994f, table 11).

Hungary, and Poland—because they have progressed the furthest and they illustrate many of the problems that the others will encounter.

The Output Decline

The most striking feature of the transition in Central Europe to date is the collapse in output that accompanied reform (table 4-2).[1] Between 1990 and 1992 GDP in the region as a whole fell more than 25 percent. Furthermore, the decline was not fully anticipated at the beginning of the process, and it was not evident in the early stages of Chinese reform. Its magnitude also seems to have little connection with the particular transition policies of individual countries. The collapse was as serious in the countries that moved slowly as in those that opted for rapid reform; and it was not more moderate in countries that had supposedly begun moving toward a market economy in prior decades, such as Hungary and Poland.

The collapse placed immediate strains on government budgets both because of the loss of revenues and the increased pressure for subsidies to distressed enterprises, greatly complicating the economic problems of these countries just at the time they were attempting to establish new democratic political systems. The reported statistics overstate the fall in economic activity because they fail to capture the

1. This issue has generated a large number of research papers in recent years and given rise to considerable controversy. See, for example, Borensztein, Demekas, and Ostry (1993); Bruno (1992); Calvo and Coricelli (1993); Nuti and Portes (1993).

full magnitude of growth in the private sector, and they do not reflect the welfare gains associated with the elimination of queuing and the introduction of greater choice in retail markets. Still, even after these adjustments, aggregate output clearly declined by large amounts throughout the region.

The slump in output is attributed to a combination of three factors: the collapse of CMEA trade, the restraint on aggregate demand required to contain inflation pressures, and the dislocations on the supply side associated with the sharp changes in the structure of relative prices and production. The reduced trade among the CMEA countries is estimated to have reduced GDP by 7–8 percent in Hungary and Czechoslovakia and about 3.5 percent in Poland.[2] When the multiplier effects on domestic incomes and demand and the disruptive effect on supplies to some industries are also taken into account, the total loss from this source is much larger. This shock was by and large associated with the decline in trade with the Soviet Union because, as discussed later, trade among the Central and East European countries was modest. Although they could purchase on the world market many of the raw materials previously obtained from Russia, they could not sell in the same market the low-quality manufactured products that Russia had formerly accepted in return.

The restrictions on demand became necessary when inflation suddenly took a sharp upward turn following the initial liberalization of domestic prices. To prevent a sustained inflationary spiral, governments imposed restraints on aggregate credit. But without the normal financial markets, there was no mechanism for allocating credit to enterprises that were economically viable but temporarily short of cash as opposed to those that could not survive under the new conditions. Most of the credit went to subsidize failing enterprises rather than to finance production.

There also is some evidence that the decline in Poland was exacerbated by excessive restraints on demand introduced to end the hyperinflation in that country.[3] Given the lack of normal market information by which to estimate the required adjustments and the uncertainties associated with any stabilization program, it is not sur-

2. Rodrik (1992b). Even higher numbers would apply to Bulgaria, which was very dependent on trade with the former Soviet Union.

3. Borensztein, Demekas, and Ostry (1993); Calvo and Coricelli (1993).

prising that the Polish stabilization program may have reduced demand more than necessary in the early stages. In particular, the authorities may have miscalculated the magnitude of the required exchange rate devaluation in early 1990, thereby adding to the domestic inflation pressures. Those effects appear to be relatively small, however, and of little lasting consequence. Furthermore, the equally large reductions in output in the other countries of the region suggest that the Polish experience was not unique as was first thought.[4]

The primary factor behind the fall in output was the disruption of the supply side of the economy. Industrial output that was economically justified under one set of relative prices became uneconomic under another. Price liberalization meant sharp increases in the price of raw material and lower prices for manufactured goods. Under the new relative price structure and the old production processes, the costs of producing many manufactured goods exceeded their value. Enterprises could not respond nor resources move quickly enough to absorb the enormous shocks that hit these economies during the price liberalization, sharply changing their comparative advantage in trade and shifting the responsibilities for managing the output of state enterprises. Similar, though less severe, are the output responses that have occurred even in advanced economies subjected to large changes in the relative price structure. All of the Central European economies had overbuilt their heavy industries, and significant amounts of their output were not marketable in the new conditions. Thus part of the decline in industrial output is a desirable effect of shifting resources to consumption, services, and trade.[5]

Since much of the decline in output is also permanent rather than cyclical, it will not turn around until new productive capacity can be developed. Large amounts of physical capital in industry have been rendered obsolete by the restructuring of output and the opening to global markets. Whereas the initial expansion of output and employment in the private sector could be concentrated in services and retail trade that did not require much capital, a major recovery of

4. Even in market economies with supposedly advanced financial and labor markets, efforts to constrain inflation pressures result in reduced output. It should not be surprising that antiinflation policies in the transitional economies imposed larger output losses.

5. China was able to avoid a similar decline in output because it did not experience a major disruption of trade, such as the collapse of the CMEA, and the more gradual introduction of price reform minimized the disruptions on the supply side of the economy. Even more important, it had a smaller and less centralized industrial sector.

industrial output will be difficult to achieve without substantial new investments.

For several of the Central European economies, the decline in aggregate output appears to be over, and they have begun a process of moderate growth. The largest economies have succeeded in achieving sufficient macroeconomic stability to begin building the micro-economic foundations of a market economy. However, the rapid growth expected at the beginning of the process still seems distant.

Domestic Reforms

Nearly all of the transitional economies started out with an exces-sive stock of money—a monetary overhang—as indicated by the prevalence of rationing and queues to constrain consumer demand. The governments decided to eliminate the overhang by simply freeing domestic prices and allowing price increases to erode the real value of existing money balances. The danger of such an approach is that it can generate pressure for compensatory wage increases that convert a one-shot rise in prices into sustained inflation. Furthermore, the asymmetric effects of inflation—which can cause government expen-ditures to rise in relation to revenues and increase the pressure for credit from enterprises adversely affected by the change in relative prices—can easily trigger successive rounds of credit creation that further fuel inflation.[6] Such inflation posed a particularly grave risk in the Central European countries because their primary source of revenue was the profits of state-owned enterprises.

The stabilization policies in this region have had mixed results. For the six countries shown in table 4-3, inflation has declined on the whole after the initial surge following price liberalization. The Czech Republic has stabilized at about a 10 percent inflation rate; in Poland, Hungary, and the Slovak Republic the rate has been about 15–30 per-cent but still allows economic reform to go forward. It is substantially higher in Bulgaria and Romania.[7] Because these countries still lack

6. An added complication in Poland was that it began its liberalization program at a time of severe macroeconomic imbalances, as indicated by the rate of inflation by 1990, which was in excess of 500 percent. OECD (1993a, table 23).

7. Controls on fuel and housing prices are still quite common, and the overall extent of government restrictions on prices is greater in Bulgaria and Romania.

Table 4-3. *Inflation in Central European Countries, 1989–94*
Rate of change

Country	Inflation					
	1989	1990	1991	1992	1993	1994[a]
Bulgaria	6	24	334	82	73	81
Czechoslovakia	1	11	59	11	. . .	. . .
Czech Republic	. . .	. . .	. . .	. . .	21	9
Slovak Republic	. . .	. . .	. . .	. . .	23	14
Hungary	17	29	34	23	22	19
Poland	251	586	70	43	35	30
Romania	1	5	161	210	256	156

Sources: IMF (1994e, table A13; 1994f, table 11).
a. Estimated.

extensive financial markets, variations in the rates of inflation are closely linked to the countries' success in containing their fiscal deficits (table 4-4). Such deficits, together with loans to state enterprises, are heavily financed through central bank credit rather than bond finance, and thus force an expansion of the money supply.

Fiscal restraint has been implemented primarily on the expenditure side because of a sharp decline in revenues associated with the falloff in the profits of state enterprises. To remedy the situation many countries have introduced value added taxes, which together with wage taxes now constitute their principal source of revenue.[8] Their dependence on profit-type taxes and wage taxes remains unsustainably high, however. Consequently, they will continue to be faced with declining revenues in future years and will have to further reduce the size of the government sector. In all of these countries, general government expenditures (outside of state enterprises) still amount to 50 percent or more of GDP.

Countries with such high rates of taxation promote the development of an informal sector predicated on tax avoidance. Poland is a prime example. It introduced an income tax in 1991 with marginal rates between 20 and 40 percent, and then instituted a 22 percent value added tax in mid-1993 to replace the previous turnover tax. It also has a 46 percent employment tax and a 40 percent tax on

8. The larger economies have introduced income taxes, but because of the administrative complexity of such a system, the amount of revenue received from this tax will be limited for several years.

Table 4-4. *General Government Balance in Central European Countries,*
1989–94
Percent of GDP

Country	General government balance					
	1989	*1990*	*1991*	*1992*	*1993*	*1994*
Bulgaria	−3.7	−8.5	−3.0	−5.7	−11.0	−8.0
Czechoslovakia	−2.4	0.1	−1.0	−3.8	. . .	. . .
Czech Republic	. . .	. . .	. . .	. . .	0.0	0.0
Slovak Republic	. . .	. . .	. . .	. . .	−8.0	−5.0
Hungary	−1.3	0.4	−2.5	−7.0	−6.0	−8.0
Poland	−7.4	3.5	−5.6	−6.9	−2.8	−4.0
Romania	8.4	1.2	0.6	−6.1	−2.0	−4.0

Sources: EBRD (1994a); OECD (1994c).

enterprise profits. These high rates, in combination with an inefficient system of tax administration, have induced an excessive degree of tax evasion. In effect the private sector remains untaxed, and much of the appeal of private activity lies in the ability to evade taxation.

Financial discipline of the enterprises, while continuing to be a significant problem, has improved, and several countries are beginning to implement programs to control intraenterprise debts and strengthen the capital structure of the banking system.[9] Even so, real money balances continue to decline and the use of foreign currencies is growing. Real rates of return on deposit accounts are often negative, and loan rates are positive, but highly volatile. New businesses have greater trouble obtaining credit, except on very restricted terms, than do the state enterprises. Several countries have experimented with debt consolidation programs, but with limited success. In general, the fiscal and financial systems are still very weak, but substantial progress has been made in a short period of time and under highly adverse conditions.

Unemployment has also risen considerably, although not as much as would have been anticipated from the drop in total output (table 4-5). The Czech Republic stands out with a particularly small

9. All of these countries drastically reduced their budgetary subsidies to the state enterprises, but in many cases the pressures were simply shifted from the budget to the financial system, which was underdeveloped and unaccustomed to regulating credit. Enterprises also extended credit to one another since the alternative was to simply turn profits over to the state.

Table 4-5. *Unemployment in Central European Countries, 1989–94*
Percent of labor force, end of year

Country	Unemployment					
	1989	1990	1991	1992	1993	1994[a]
Bulgaria	0.0	1.6	11.7	15.2	16.3	13.0
Czechoslovakia	0.0	1.0	6.8	5.1	. . .	. . .
Czech Republic	. . .	. . .	. . .	. . .	3.5	4.0
Slovak Republic	. . .	. . .	. . .	. . .	14.4	14.0
Hungary	0.3	1.6	7.5	12.3	12.2	11.0
Poland	0.1	6.1	11.5	13.6	15:7	17.0
Romania	0.0	0.0	2.7	8.4	10.2	11.0

Sources: OECD (1994c); IMF (1994f, table 13).
a. Preliminary data.

increase. In general, industrial employment has fallen by 20–30 percent. This decline has been partly offset by the rapid growth of private sector jobs in retail trade and services, but that reallocation may slow down once the size of the trade sector, which had been repressed, expands to a more normal share of overall employment. Furthermore, there is still a large amount of excess labor within the state enterprises. Several studies have found a surprisingly high level of labor mobility as workers move from the state-owned enterprises to private firms and also within the state sector, but the movement from unemployment to employment is quite low.[10] In the Czech Republic, for example, almost one-half of the labor force experienced a change of employment in 1991–92.[11] Employment in the private sector remains unattractive, however, in that wage rates are generally below those of the state-owned firms.

The privatization of the state enterprises has proceeded more slowly than was originally intended. One reason is that none of these countries have enough private wealth to purchase the enterprises. The experience of Chile and others suggests that allowing the use of credit to finance takeovers can lead to perverse management incentives and a dangerous degree of financial instability. At the same time, all of the countries except Hungary are strongly opposed to giving foreign investors an extensive role in the conversion process. Nor are foreigners particularly interested in purchasing an existing enterprise

10. Blanchard, Commander, and Coricelli (1995).
11. OECD (1994b, p. 69).

when they have the option of starting a new one. The Czech Republic, where the process of privatization has moved forward at a rapid pace, stands out as an exception.

Although privatization of the large firms has been moving at a slow pace, this has not proved costly to the process, to date. In contrast, the privatization of small establishments, particularly in the retail trade, has been very rapid, and the large state firms have sharply reduced the size of their work force. Poland now has the largest private sector, at about 60 percent of total employment, followed by about one-third in the Czech and Slovak republics. Thus employment is adjusting, despite continued state ownership. Also, there is evidence that the performance of many state enterprises is improving and that budgetary constraints on the enterprises are gradually being tightened, as witnessed by the declining levels of employment.[12]

Several of the Central European countries have already implemented a large proportion of the economic reforms required to convert to market-based economies. Thus most production decisions are now based on price signals, and privatization programs are going forward. Many of the most pressing current problems are not much different from those faced by developing countries: an underdeveloped financial system and difficulty controlling the government budget, with the result that accelerating inflation is a constant threat. The trauma of the past few years has had a political cost in that the population has voted for new governments that propose to slow the process of change. However, there is little evidence that the course adopted at the beginning of the decade is being reversed. More significant is the extent to which the countries of the region have diverged. Hungary, Poland, the Czech and Slovak Republics, and Slovenia appear to have taken most of the steps required to move to a market economy and now face a more traditional set of problems in promoting economic growth. Others, such as Bulgaria and Romania, are lagging further behind.

External Economic Relations

The pace of change has been most dramatic in the area of foreign economic relations. Before 1990, as discussed in chapter 1, the

---

12. Pinto, Belka, and Krajewski (1993).

CMEA countries barely interacted with the global economy. Trade was a small share of GDP, was administered by state agencies in nonconvertible currencies, and was dominated by trade with the former Soviet Union, which accounted for about two-thirds of CMEA trade. Since 1990, the larger Central European states have made their currencies convertible for current account transactions, eliminated the state monopoly over trade, established a system of relatively low and uniform tariffs, and all but eliminated most restrictions on exports. In the case of some countries, such as Poland and Hungary, several of the trade-liberalizing measures were initiated in the 1980s, but they had little effect until they were combined with liberalization on the domestic front and could thereby affect prices there and the incentives faced by the enterprises.

Most of these countries have avoided the pressure to use tariffs and quotas as a major tool of industrial policy. Some still favor protection as a means of providing time for enterprises to adjust whereas others are concerned that it would reduce the incentives to undertake adjustment.[13] In any case, few Central European countries appear to have designed their tariff structures with protection as a main goal. Rather, the rates are quite uniform, with higher rates generally applying to consumption goods.[14] Tariffs were low to begin with, and the more significant step they took to liberalize trade was to eliminate licensing requirements and other forms of direct state control over trade. In part, tariff protection seemed redundant in view of the severely depreciated currencies, and tariffs have been more important as a temporary source of revenue. Sector policies are also difficult to design because of the extreme nature of changes in comparative advantage that accompanied the reforms.

There have been major changes on the opposite side of the market as well, that is, in terms of increased access to Western markets. The OECD countries have extended the generalized system of preferences (GSP) to cover the six leading economies of Central Europe, have

13. It has been pointed out that Central Europe differs from the usual case of "infant industry" protection in that protection there is more for "senile industries." See Williamson (1991).

14. Average tariff rates are generally between 10 and 20 percent for the six major Central European economies. Czechoslovakia initially set tariffs at the low average of 5 percent, but they were later increased. There has been some tendency for tariffs to rise in response to pressures on the balance of payments.

granted them most-favored-nation status, and narrowed the role of previous trade laws regarding state trading. Most important, the European Union entered into association agreements that call for the phasing-in of free trade over a ten-year period. The reduction of tariffs and quotas is asymmetric in that the union immediately reduced trade restrictions and is committed to eliminating such barriers within the first five years, while the Central European countries can maintain some protection until the later years of the transition. However, the union has introduced special provisions for a set of sensitive sectors—food, textiles and apparel, iron and steel, and chemicals— that at present account for about one-third of the manufacturing sector in the countries of Central Europe.[15] The United States extended most-favored-nation status to Central Europe but maintained apparel quotas. Agreements have also been signed with the European Free Trade Association to move toward free trade over the 1990s. The countries of Central Europe remain susceptible to antidumping charges from the United States and Europe, with consequent pressures to accede to various forms of voluntary restraints on exports in categories of sensitive products.[16]

The association agreements have been criticized by those who would like to see a faster move to full membership in the European Union. However, to compare their entry to that of other countries, such as Spain, ignores the fact that the others entered the union at a much earlier stage of its integration and that their adjustment to free trade, complete capital account convertibility, and the single market stretched over decades. It seems that full membership is unlikely to come in the near future because of the large costs it would impose on other members, who would be required to finance the Common Agricultural Policy and structural adjustment program, and because it would necessitate a slower pace of deep integration of the union.[17] Membership would, however, greatly increase the flow of private

15. One problem with the association agreements is that they have not been matched with similar agreements among the countries of Central Europe. As Baldwin (1994, pp. 130–39) points out, they stand as independent spokes in a system in which the European Union is the hub. The barriers to trade across the spokes makes them less attractive as production bases for the European Union.

16. Additional details on the agreements are provided in EBRD (1993, pp. 17–24).

17. Baldwin (1994). Of course, outsiders might favor the move precisely because it would force the countries to abandon their highly protectionist agricultural system.

Table 4-6. *Average Monthly Dollar Wage in Central European Economies, 1990–93*

Economy	1990	1991	1992	1993
Bulgaria	136	63	96	125
Czechoslovakia[a]	198	139	169	205
Hungary	214	233	278	298
Poland	139	209	222	235
Romania	176	143	87	102
Western Europe, Four[b]	2,037	2,120	2,293	2,127
Asian NIEs[c]	532	608	685	734

Sources: PlanEcon (1994a, p. 25); U.S. Department of Labor, Bureau of Labor Statistics, unpublished data.

a. Data for Czech Republic.

b. Average of France, Germany, Great Britain, and Italy.

c. Hong Kong, South Korea, Singapore, and Taiwan. The data are for the manufacturing sector.

capital to the region by sharply reducing the perception of risks now associated with such investments.

All of these countries have greatly depreciated real exchange rates, with the result that Central Europe has become a source of exceptionally cheap labor. As shown in table 4-6, wage rates among the larger Central European countries were only about 10 percent of the Western European levels in 1992 and about one-third of the levels in the Asian NIEs.[18] The magnitude of this cost advantage is a powerful incentive for export, but also a measure of the tremendous gap in production and marketing technologies between the East and the West. Effective labor costs rose in 1993 because of a general tendency toward real exchange rate appreciation (see table 4-7). Nevertheless, the wage differentials remain very large. For Bulgaria and Romania, the continuing decline in the exchange rate is a reflection of their inability to achieve macroeconomic stability, but in general low real exchange rates (in relation to purchasing power parity) predate the reforms. Hungary and Poland have both seen their real exchange rates rise since 1990.

18. The low wage costs are somewhat overstated in the statistics, which exclude employment taxes and the costs of the benefit programs provided by state-owned enterprises. Nonwage compensation is a larger portion of total compensation in the countries of Central Europe than in the other countries. However, the adjustment would not change the conclusion that wage rates for workers with equivalent skills are much lower in the East.

Table 4-7. *The Real Exchange Rate, Central European Countries, 1989–93*
Percent of purchasing power parity (PPP)

Country	1989	1990	1991	1992	1993
Bulgaria	46.7	14.9	6.1	18.7	28.0
Czechoslovakia[a]	44.1	38.4	35.7	39.7	45.0
Hungary	50.1	57.2	62.7	70.7	69.7
Poland	35.0	33.2	50.4	55.3	55.3
Romania	99.1	65.4	49.5	25.8	25.8

Sources: Calculated by the authors using annual averages of the nominal exchange rate adjusted by changes in consumer prices relative to the United States. The PPP exchange rate is computed from table 1-2. Data are from IMF (1994c); EBRD (1994a, table 2, p. 118); OECD (1994d, p. 25); OECD (1994e, p. 25).

a. Data for Czech Republic for 1993.

Trade Performance

The liberalization of the trade regime, devaluation, and the collapse of domestic demand created strong incentives for export; and with the termination of the CMEA, any expansion of trade had to be with the West. Indeed, this is the direction trade has taken.

Overall, total trade for most of the Central European countries has contracted greatly (table 4-8). Only Poland reports a nominal dollar level of exports for 1993 that exceeds the level of 1989. The trade statistics from this region are difficult to interpret, however, because few countries had an adequate system for recording trade flows at the outset. The data situation is further complicated by the breakup of the CMEA and the fact that a large portion of trade before 1991 was in nonconvertible currencies. Cross-rates between the ruble and the dollar are generally used to estimate trade in nonconvertible currencies. Corresponding reports of partner countries can at least be used to confirm trends in trade performance. The data from partner countries suggest that significant amounts of imports and exports are not being captured by the national statistical systems. Furthermore, the aggregate trade data do not reflect the sharp restructuring of trade that is occurring, both in geographic and product composition.

As shown in table 4-9, exports from Czechoslovakia, Hungary, and Poland to the industrial countries rose by 55 percent between 1989 and 1992, according to their own trade statistics, and rose by 88 percent according to partner-country data.[19] Imports from the indus-

19. The direction of trade statistics is not available for Bulgaria and Romania.

Table 4-8. *Change in Exports and Imports of Central European Countries,*
1990–93
Percentage change in U.S. dollar values

Country	1990	1991	1992	1993[a]	1989–1993
Exports					
Bulgaria[b]	−26.1	−38.9	36.3	−20.0	−51.0
Czechoslovakia	−18.2	−8.9	8.2	5.3[c]	−15.0
Hungary	−12.8	5.9	4.2	−19.6	−23.0
Poland	23.1	−9.1	−3.2	−3.1	4.8
Romania	−44.0	−27.3	2.3	12.1	−53.4
Imports					
Bulgaria[b]	−17.1	−49.3	+22.3	−20.0	−58.8
Czechoslovakia	−7.2	−17.9	24.1	3.6[c]	−2.1
Hungary	−8.8	8.3	8.4	10.2	17.9
Poland	−4.5	23.3	−6.9	18.5	29.9
Romania	8.0	−41.1	7.7	−4.1	−28.6

Sources: IMF (1994a; 1994c).

a. 1993 data are preliminary.

b. 1993 data are estimated on the basis of data from IMF (1994b).

c. Estimates of the 1993 trade of the combined Czech and Slovak republics were calculated using data from the OECD (1994b, pp. 48, 56) and the EBRD (1994a, pp. 125, 127).

trial countries also appear to have been significantly underreported: they increased by 82 percent in their own statistics and by 122 percent in partner-country data. All of the growth in exports was to Western Europe, particularly to Germany, which has emerged as the region's dominant trading partner. Germany accounts for more than a fourth of total exports and imports. Although trade with Western Europe began from a low base, less than 10 percent of GDP, a near doubling within four years is an impressive performance. It still represents a trivial portion of total imports of the European Union: less than 2 percent.

The increased trade with the West was offset by an equally large collapse of trade with the rest of Central Europe and the countries of the former Soviet Union. Because this trade did not involve convertible currencies before 1990, its precise valuation is uncertain, but the decline of exports was about 50 percent. Imports from Russia were sustained by the continued purchase of energy and raw materials. The share of the former CMEA in total trade declined from 35 percent in 1989 to 21 percent in 1992.

Table 4-9. *Structure of Trade of Czechoslovakia, Hungary, and Poland, 1989–93*
Billions of U.S. dollars

Region	Exports, f.o.b.					Imports, c.i.f. [a]				
	1989	1990	1991	1992	1993	1989	1990	1991	1992	1993
IFS balance of payments	37.6	36.6	34.7	35.5	n.a.	36.3	33.9	35.2	37.5	n.a.
DOTS, world total	37.3	34.9	35.8	36.2	34.7	33.3	30.0	36.9	42.5	46.0
Central Europe[b]	4.7	3.2	2.9	2.7	2.1	4.6	3.8	2.3	2.1	2.0
Former USSR	9.6	7.0	5.0	4.5	3.7	8.5	6.4	7.3	7.7	6.5
Industrial countries[c]	16.0	19.1	23.3	24.2	23.8	15.5	16.8	22.5	24.8	31.8
Europe	14.5	17.8	22.0	22.8	22.3	14.5	15.7	20.8	22.5	29.1
Other	1.4	1.3	1.3	1.4	1.5	1.0	1.0	1.7	2.3	2.7
Rest of world	7.0	5.5	4.7	4.8	5.0	4.7	3.0	4.8	7.9	5.7
Partner countries data[d]										
The world	41.2	38.2	36.2	38.6	36.5	37.0	33.3	40.0	41.6	44.8
Industrial countries	14.5	19.7	22.9	27.3	25.9	14.4	20.4	26.0	31.9	33.5

Source: IMF (1994b, 1994d). Data refer to the former Czechoslovakia, Hungary, and Poland. IFS is *International Financial Statistics* and DOTS is *Direction of Trade Statistics*.

n.a. Not available.

a. IFS balance-of-payments import data are f.o.b.

b. Central Europe includes Bulgaria, Czechoslovakia, Hungary, Poland, and Romania; Slovak Republic data for 1993 are estimated.

c. Includes both East and West Germany.

d. Exports are c.i.f. (cost, insurance, and freight) and imports are f.o.b. (freight on board).

Equally large changes are evident in the product composition of trade. Before 1990, Central Europe's exports to the Soviet Union were heavily concentrated in machinery, whereas trade with the West was oriented toward agriculture, chemicals, and basic manufactures.[20] Machinery products initially were not considered marketable in the West because of quality problems, and in any case export expansion was expected to concentrate on agricultural products and basic manufactures. Yet the growth of exports to the European Union has been strongest in machinery and miscellaneous manufacturing (table 4-10).[21] The latter category is largely apparel and footwear, reflecting the current comparative advantage in products using low-wage labor. These countries have done better than expected in the more complex machine products, and it appears that some of the previous exports to the CMEA are being redirected to the West.[22] Large increases are also reported for semimanufactured products. For the most part, the percentage expansion of agricultural exports and basic materials, such as steel and chemicals, has been quite modest, probably because of restrictions on imports of these sensitive products into the European Union.

On the import side, the largest increases have been in fuels, machinery, and basic manufactures.[23] The growth of machinery imports is encouraging in that it is consistent with the use of export earnings to purchase more advanced capital equipment from the West as part of enterprise restructuring. Although detailed data are lacking, the growth of manufacturing trade on both the import and export side also implies an increase in intraindustry trade and some progress in integrating these countries into a European production network.

The trade performance of Czechoslovakia, Hungary, and Poland differs markedly from that of Bulgaria and Romania. Bulgaria was very severely affected by the collapse of CMEA trade, and at first it

20. Some details on the product composition of trade with the CMEA and the West in 1989 are provided in table 4-A1. Additional data on the change in trade between Central Europe and the OECD are provided in table 4-A2.

21. We have used partner-country data on the composition of trade because of the incomplete nature of the reports from the transitional economies.

22. This conclusion is disputed by Rodrik (1992a), but his data were largely limited to 1990.

23. The commodity composition of imports of Czechoslovakia, Hungary, and Poland from the OECD countries are shown in table 4-A2.

Table 4-10. *Percentage Change in Merchandise Exports to the European Union and Contribution of Major Product Groups, 1989–92*

Percent

Product group	Bulgaria		Czechoslovakia		Hungary		Poland		Romania	
	Percent change	Contribution	Percent change	Contribution	Percent change	Contribution	Percent change	Contribution	Percent change	Contribution
Total	95.3	95.3	153.7	153.7	82.3	82.3	114.5	114.5	−33.0	−33.0
Primary products	56.8	24.5	44.5	13.0	28.7	11.7	51.9	26.5	−83.0	−36.0
Manufactures	134.5	72.5	200.7	137.9	121.0	69.8	181.3	86.9	4.5	2.5
Iron and steel	11.3	1.2	102.5	12.8	23.6	1.1	85.0	4.5	−4.4	−0.2
Chemicals	37.1	4.4	92.1	10.7	80.5	8.0	130.1	8.6	−24.8	−1.1
Other semi-manufactures	212.0	8.9	289.1	32.7	129.5	9.4	259.2	19.9	−18.6	−1.4
Machinery and transport	101.4	11.9	277.4	38.6	174.4	22.2	143.2	16.9	−8.8	−0.5
Textiles	119.0	4.2	107.3	6.8	54.1	1.6	134.2	2.3	−9.1	−0.1
Clothing	365.9	27.0	316.2	14.5	127.4	14.8	244.7	21.4	37.6	6.1
Other consumer goods	303.3	15.2	258.8	21.8	152.3	12.6	219.8	13.4	0.7	0.1
Other products (not elsewhere classified)	−55.6	−1.7	132.8	2.9	53.3	0.8	102.1	1.1	500.0	0.5

Sources: GATT (1993, p. 25); and authors' calculations. The contribution of a subcomponent is measured as its percent change multiplied by its share of the total in 1989.

Table 4-11. *Current Account Balances, Central European Countries,*
1990–94
Billions of U.S. dollars

Country	1990	1991	1992	1993	1994 (est.)
Bulgaria	−1.2	−0.9	−0.7	−1.4	−1.2
Czechoslovakia	−1.1	0.4	0.2	. . .	. . .
Czech Republic	. . .	. . .	. . .	0.4	0.1
Slovak Republic	. . .	. . .	. . .	0.1	0.1
Hungary	0.1	0.3	0.3	−2.0	−2.5
Poland[a]	0.7	−1.4	−1.5	−1.7	−1.6
Romania	−1.7	−1.4	−1.5	−1.7	−1.6
Total	−3.1	−3.1	−2.0	−6.6	−7.3
Net interest payments	n.a.	−5.0	−3.4	−2.8	−3.5

Source: OECD (1993b, table 25).

a. The IMF reports substantially higher deficits for 1991 and 1992: $2.3 and $2.7 billion, respectively. Under the IMF approach, the current account includes the full interest commitments on official debt; the 80 percent reduction of interest for three years is an element of the Paris Club agreement and is treated as a capital transaction. The figures reported here treat it as a simple reduction of interest commitments, thereby showing a current account balance that is less negative.

moved more slowly than the others to reform its trade system. Exports to the West did expand, but from a very low base. Romania had previously had a high level of trade with the West, but it was based on a distorted notion of comparative advantage. Romania was processing heavily subsidized energy and other raw material imports from the Soviet Union and selling the products for hard currency in the West. With the movement to world prices for trade among the CMEA countries, those exports became uneconomic. In general, there appears to be a positive relationship between the speed and completeness of the domestic reforms and the extent of export growth.

Interestingly, the Czech and Slovak republics have done as well as, or better than, Poland and Hungary in expanding their trade with Western Europe, despite the fact that their reforms were far less advanced at the beginning of the 1990s. Apparently both Poland and Hungary obtained few benefits from having undertaken extensive trade liberalization in the 1980s; and, at least in this case, the length of the adjustment period mattered less than supposed.

Export growth weakened in 1993 and 1994, and current account deficits increased (tables 4-8 and 4-11). In part, this trend reflects an appreciation of real exchange rates and a deterioration in their competitive position. As shown in table 4-7, real exchange rates rose between 1990 and 1993 in the three major economies, but they are still well below PPP levels, and, as shown in table 4-6, labor costs are still very low. Thus cost increases are probably not the full explanation. These economies were hard hit by the 1992–93 recession in Western Europe, which has emerged as their principal export market. Their involvement with markets outside Europe is now limited. Furthermore, the compression of domestic demand created a strong incentive to export in the 1990–92 period, often at greatly reduced prices. An improving domestic economic situation has weakened some of those incentives.

Continued low levels of foreign direct investment indicate that Central Europe has not yet emerged as an attractive production base for multinational firms, as China has. Investors are not yet confident that they will find stable commercial environments in the region because tax rates and regulations continually change, and the expected shift of production from the West to the East, to take advantage of low labor costs, has not yet occurred on a large scale. One major problem is that the Central European countries have yet to establish adequate administrative systems for collecting taxes. In effect, much of the private sector activity is untaxed, and the tax burden falls heavily on the state enterprises and foreign firms that are highly visible to the tax administrators. Unlike China, the Central European states have not extended highly favorable tax concessions to foreign firms. Although they are generally accorded national treatment, that is not very favorable in view of the high tax rates.

At present, the greatest barriers to the expansion of trade lie within the domestic economies of these countries. Difficulties with the communications and transportation infrastructure are the most frequently cited problems of companies engaged in trade.[24] In addition, the processing of trade at the border creates long delays.

Capital Account Financing

The transitional economies have received a surprisingly small amount of external financial assistance to date; and the limited amount of private direct investment is far short of the expected levels.

24. OECD (1994a).

Since the countries began the transition with very low levels of foreign exchange reserves, they have been forced to finance the restructuring out of their own export earnings and to use a depreciated currency as the primary means of generating exports.

A summary of financial flows into the region is provided in table 4-12. Until 1993, there was actually a resource transfer out of the region as these countries were required to generate trade surpluses in order to service the debt run up by the prior regimes. Bulgaria, Hungary, and Poland have significant amounts of external debt. Hungary has been able to meet its scheduled repayments; but Bulgaria and Poland have frequently been in arrears and have been involved in several debt restructurings in the 1990s. The exceptional finance line of table 4-12 reflects changes in arrears and debt restructuring.[25] In addition, all of these countries had very low reserves when they moved to convertibility, and they set aside about $10 billion of foreign exchange over the 1991–93 period as additions to reserves.

Net external financing averaged $6.5 billion a year, or 3–5 percent of GDP in the 1991–93 period, with the bulk of those funds coming from foreign direct investment. About a third of this investment was associated with the privatization of state enterprises, and the bulk of it went to Hungary. The International Monetary Fund and the World Bank also provided about $10 billion of transitional financing in 1990–93. The magnitude of assistance from the multilateral organizations, as a percentage of GDP, has been about three times that provided to the average developing country. Official bilateral grants and loans have been small, however, and privately supplied debt has actually declined. Traditional bank loans have also been a minor source of finance, but both Hungary and the Czech Republic were able to raise significant amounts of funds in the international bond market in 1993: $0.9 and $5 billion respectively. Thus far, the problems Poland has had in financing its existing debt have prevented it from raising private capital in international markets. Overall, the annual flow of external financing to Central Europe has been about one-third the flow to China, but the countries are at an earlier stage of their transition programs.

25. The differing estimates of the current account deficit in tables 4-11 and 4-12 reflect alternative ways of treating interest payments. In table 4-12 the current account is measured on the basis of scheduled interest, rather than actual payments, and debt restructurings are treated as a capital account transaction.

Table 4-12. *External Financing: Six Major Central European Economies,*
1988–93[a]

Billions of U.S. dollars

Category	1988	1989	1990	1991	1992	1993
Balance: goods and services	6.8	4.0	−0.8	0.4	0.2	−7.9
(+) Net factor income	−4.9	−5.2	−5.6	−4.3	−5.6	−4.9
(+) Private transfers	2.0	1.9	3.4	1.7	1.2	1.7
(=) Current account, excluding official transfers	4.0	0.6	−3.1	−2.2	−4.2	−11.1
(+) Reserve change (− = increase)	−0.8	−1.5	1.6	−4.4	−2.1	−3.6
(+) Exceptional finance	3.9	3.6	−0.8	5.3	4.9	3.5
(+) Asset transactions, including errors and omissions[b]	−5.4	−3.4	1.4	−6.3	−3.2	3.8
(=) Net financial balance	1.6	−0.7	−0.9	−7.6	−4.6	−7.5
Net external financing	−1.6	0.7	0.9	7.6	4.6	7.5
(−) Official transfers	−0.0	0.1	0.4	0.3	0.4	0.3
(−) Direct investment	−0.0	0.3	0.3	2.4	3.3	5.0
(=) Net external borrowing[c]	−1.5	0.4	0.3	4.9	0.9	2.1
IMF credits	−0.5	−0.3	0.4	3.7	0.7	0.1
Short-term debt	0.7	0.4	−1.0	−0.9	−1.0	−0.5
Long-term debt	−1.8	0.3	0.9	2.1	1.1	2.5
Official creditors	−1.2	−1.1	0.5	2.1	2.1	3.0
Multilateral	−0.5	−0.6	0.6	1.7	1.7	...
Bilateral	−0.7	−0.5	−0.1	0.3	0.5	...
Private creditors	−0.6	1.5	0.4	0.0	−1.0	−0.5
Addenda						
Debt amortization	9.1	7.1	4.4	3.8	4.9	4.5
Total debt	80.9	82.6	91.1	99.5	95.4	...
Percentage of GDP	38.9	37.6	47.3	55.6	50.6	...

Sources: IMF (1994a); World Bank (1993d); authors' estimates.

a. The six economies are Bulgaria, the Czech Republic, the Slovak Republic, Hungary, Poland, and Romania.

b. Residually derived by subtracting net external finance and the items identified above from the current account balance.

c. Obtained from IMF (1993d). Debt changes are reported net of amortizations.

Somewhat larger estimates of financial assistance are given by the IMF, which reports the level to be about $14 billion a year.[26] Its measures are based on a broader concept that includes debt relief, nonconcessional trade credit extended by exporters to the Central European nations, and payments to their own nationals who serve as consultants. These actions have not translated into significant net resource transfers into the region. Although debt relief reduced the payment arrears of Poland, it has not yet translated into a net inflow of funds.

Future Steps

Most of the regulatory and institutional structure these countries require to participate in the global trading system in goods is now in place. The major Central European economies have current account convertibility and a relatively uniform and transparent tariff system. The future growth in trade will be more dependent on a deepening of the links between individual enterprises and the external market than on changes in rules and institutions. That is, they have moved from the transition stage of institution building to one in which the emphasis must be on investments in products suitable for sale in the international market. These countries will also require several years of large investments to bring their communications and transportation systems up to the standards of Western Europe.

They have moved less rapidly to integrate the service sector with the international economy. Although their domestic financial systems remain too fragile to support full capital account convertibility, these countries could improve the commercial environment for foreign activity in services. The commercial sectors are particularly underdeveloped. Because of the lack of a significant prior involvement of domestic firms, there should be less concern with a large foreign role in finance and business services. A high degree of integration with Western Europe in these sectors would complement exports of goods by improving the flow of information on regulations governing health and safety, packaging, and marketing skills.

The most significant external issue concerns their future relationship with the European Union. The association agreements stop short

26. IMF (1994e, p. 76).

of even free trade because of the importance of potential trade in the "sensitive" sectors. Yet, the European Union cannot proceed with full membership for these countries while maintaining protective restraints in these sectors. It cannot afford, for example, to grant full membership while maintaining the Common Agricultural Policy (CAP), because of greatly expanded fiscal costs. Yet, as shown by the recent GATT negotiations, many current members are strongly opposed to scaling back the CAP. Furthermore, the issue of the membership of these countries in the European Union will force union members to decide whether they want a deeper integration—particularly in the financial sphere—or a wider but shallower structure. Full membership in the European Union would provide these countries with a degree of stability and credibility that could greatly increase the flow of foreign direct investment and the technological modernization that would accompany it.

Conclusion

As far as most expectations at the beginning of the decade are concerned, the economic transition of the Central European countries has been a disappointment. It has proved to be more difficult and will stretch out over a much longer period than originally thought. Unlike China, economic reform in Central Europe was accompanied by large reductions in output and employment. Yet in retrospect it is those early expectations that seem most out of line. When the magnitude of change that had to be undertaken is taken into account, these countries have actually made enormous progress. In fact, some countries—such as the Czech Republic, Hungary, and Poland—have by and large completed the institutional changes required in a transition to market economies. This is not to deny that they have a long way to go in privatizing the state enterprises, developing an effective domestic financial system, and reforming the structure of public finance. However, measurable progress has been made in all of these areas, and it is increasingly evident that the benefits of privatizating existing enterprises will be more in the form of relieving a burden than providing a direct stimulus to growth. Like many developing economies, these countries have yet to deepen their market institutions and develop effective strategies to promote economic growth. That means maintaining macroeconomic stability and promoting a recovery of domestic rates of saving and capital formation. These problems are hardly unique to the region.

At the level of trade in goods and services, substantial progress has also been made in integrating these countries into the world economy. An early move to current account convertibility succeeded in promoting a rapid growth in non-CMEA trade. The sharp increases in exports to Western Europe would seem to belie the argument that they would be unable to gain access to these markets. Instead, limitations on exports seem to be more related to the speed of domestic adjustment and to the development of effective export products. Market access does not seem to be a serious problem beyond a group of sensitive products in which the industrial countries have limited imports from all sources.

Trade liberalization was expensive for these countries in that it initally made domestic price stabilization more complicated. Under the extremely low real exchange rates of the early years of the transition, the price of imported goods pushed up domestic prices instead of imposing restraints on monopolistic domestic producers, as was originally expected. Over the longer term, however, convertibility provides the basis for a more rational restructuring of industry, and the added exports have provided the financing needed to purchase modern capital equipment for restructuring. On balance, the quick move to current account convertibility seems to have been the right decision.

These countries have not attempted to establish capital account convertibility (except for foreign direct investment), but that is in accord with standard interpretations of the experience of other countries. Complete liberalization of external financial transactions requires well-developed domestic financial markets, sufficient foreign exchange reserves, and a credible economic policy to prevent episodes of capital flight and speculation. In practice, there are significant leakages in the capital controls, but they do reduce the volatility of capital movements.

One large disappointment for these countries has been their inability to attract foreign capital. Again, it is the earlier expectations that seem most unrealistic.[27] China, for instance, did not begin to receive

27. Expectations of large capital inflows into Central Europe were most prominent in discussions at the beginning of the decade of a looming global capital shortage and projections of annual capital flows to Central Europe in excess of $100 billion. See CEPR (1990).

large amounts of foreign direct investment until nearly a decade after it began its reform program, and several years after it liberalized the external trade sector. Most investors remain uncertain about the permanence of the institutional changes in Central Europe, but in future years foreign activity seems bound to grow to take advantage of the extremely low labor costs. In this case, the pattern would seem to be strikingly similar to that in Spain after its entry into the European Union.

More financial assistance to these countries would obviously help reduce their social costs and speed up economic growth. Similar arguments could be made for many developing countries, however, and care should be taken to ensure that any increase in financial aid is not simply a diversion from other developing regions of the globe. At this point the economies of Central Europe resemble other developing countries far more than they do the countries of postwar Europe, to which they are frequently compared. There is little reason to believe that capital inflows would yield benefits in excess of those available elsewhere. What they need most are inflows of direct investment that would be accompanied by improved technologies, management skills, and assistance in marketing in the global economy. Whether they will be successful in this regard will depend on developments in the domestic economy.

Integration with the global economy has also proceeded rapidly at the institutional level. The Central Europeans have become members of the leading international economic institutions, and they have taken important steps toward a deeper integration with Western Europe, through the signing of agreements with the European Union and EFTA. Although the initial efforts to develop the rules of a market economy were surrounded by considerable political conflict, the three major economies in the region have made steady progress in bringing their regulatory systems into line with those of Western Europe.

Table 4-A1. *Commodity Distribution of Exports and Imports, Czechoslovakia, Hungary, and Poland, 1989*
Percent of total

Commodity	Exports			Imports			Trade balance (millions of dollars)		
	Central Europe	USSR	Other	Central Europe	USSR	Other	Central Europe	USSR	Other
Food and live animals	3.4	6.2	14.1	3.1	0.7	12.2	19	528	762
Crude materials	3.4	3.1	7.9	3.9	8.8	11.1	-32	-400	-390
Mineral fuels	4.1	3.3	8.1	4.6	51.0	2.7	-31	-3,695	1,243
Chemicals	6.8	7.1	10.1	8.6	4.5	15.7	-115	308	-767
Basic manufactures	13.5	9.2	26.1	12.6	8.7	16.1	58	174	2,641
Iron and steel	3.0	2.8	8.5	2.2	2.8	3.2	57	38	1,253
Other basic manufactures	10.5	6.4	17.6	10.5	5.9	12.9	1	136	1,387
Machines and transport equipment	55.0	55.2	23.5	53.1	24.3	33.1	127	3,229	-1,170
Transport	9.8	11.3	4.4	9.3	2.8	3.1	31	833	377
Other machinery	45.2	43.9	19.1	43.8	21.5	30.1	96	2,396	-1,547
Miscellaneous manufactured goods	7.9	12.2	7.6	8.5	1.3	8.7	-33	1,032	4
Clothing	1.2	6.0	3.4	1.4	0.0	3.3	-13	556	115
Other manufactures	6.8	6.2	4.2	7.1	1.3	5.4	-20	476	-111
Goods not classed by kind	5.9	3.6	2.5	5.7	0.8	0.4	17	274	467
Total, percent	100	100	100	100	100	100	...	...	...
Total, U.S. dollars	1,590	2,468	9,519	1,349	1,655	7,273	10	1,450	2,790

Source: United Nations (1994). Other includes Czechoslovakia, Hungary, and Poland. Eastern Europe includes Albania, Bulgaria, Czechoslovakia, German Democratic Republic, Hungary, Poland, and Romania.

Table 4-A2. *Change in the Commodity Distribution of Exports to and Imports from the OECD, CEEC-3, 1989*
Millions of U.S. dollars

Commodity	Exports				Imports				Trade balance			
	1989	*1992*	*Change*	*Percent change*	*1989*	*1992*	*Change*	*Percent change*	*1989*	*1992*	*Change*	*Percent change*
Food and live animals	2,531	2,922	391	15	1,147	1,899	752	66	1,384	1,023	-361	-26
Crude materials	1,565	2,329	764	49	961	1,212	251	26	604	1,117	513	85
Mineral fuels	1,565	1,767	202	13	135	1,209	1,074	796	1,430	558	-872	-61
Chemicals	1,436	2,300	864	60	2,534	3,977	1,443	57	-1,098	-1,677	-579	53
Basic manufactures	3,406	7,065	3,659	107	2,576	5,743	3,167	123	830	1,322	492	59
Iron and steel	1,028	1,587	559	54	484	593	109	23	544	994	450	83
Other basic manufactures	2,378	5,478	3,100	130	2,092	5,150	3,058	146	286	328	42	15
Machines and transport equipment	1,923	4,889	2,966	154	5,457	13,232	7,775	142	-3,534	-8,343	-4,809	136
Transport	524	1,637	1,113	212	893	3,605	2,712	304	-369	-1,968	-1,599	433
Other machinery	1,399	3,252	1,853	132	4,564	9,627	5,063	111	-3,165	-6,375	-3,210	101
Miscellaneous manufactured goods	2,125	5,934	3,809	179	1,244	3,057	1,813	146	881	2,877	1,996	227
Clothing	1,347	3,790	2,443	181	289	1,005	716	248	1,058	2,785	1,727	163
Other manufactures	778	2,144	1,366	176	955	2,052	1,097	115	-177	92	269	-152
Goods not classed by kind	142	273	131	92	231	417	186	81	-89	-144	-55	62
Total	14,693	27,479	12,786	87	14,285	30,746	16,461	115	-84	508	592	-705

Sources: OECD (1990) and data provided to authors by OECD staff. Data refer to the former Czechoslovakia, Hungary, and Poland (CEEC-3).

Chapter 5

Conclusion

*T*O DATE, the former socialist countries have had highly variable results from their economic reforms. China stands out for having achieved a rate of growth close to 10 percent a year since beginning its reforms in the late 1970s. All of the other transitional economies have experienced very large declines in output and incomes in the early years of the transition. For the major Central European economies, the future still looks hopeful, however, as they have completed the basic institutional reforms, established a fair degree of stability in their fiscal and monetary policies, and are beginning a process of positive economic growth. In contrast, the situation remains grim for the countries of the former Soviet Union and some other countries in Central and Eastern Europe.

It is also evident that the liberalization of the foreign trade sector has been an important element of the overall reform program, and that those countries that sought to enter the global economy have been quite successful in developing markets for their exports in the West. Their overall trade response has been disappointing only because of the collapse of their trade with one another. Except for China, they have done less well in attracting the interest of Western investors who might provide the financing and technical knowledge needed to modernize their economies. The lack of private sector interest seems closely related to uncertainties about the domestic economic situation, particularly the shaky commercial environment. Finally, Western governments have done less than expected to help with the transition in view of the importance they attached to ending the cold war.

147

China is an amazing economic success story, but it is also a special case of economic transition. Unlike the other former socialist economies, it did not have an overdeveloped industrial sector. The structure of its markets for agricultural products was simpler than that for industrial products, and the liberalization of prices brought a fast response on the supply side in the agricultural sector. Because state enterprises played a small role in the economy, China could afford to postpone privatizing them and could focus on developing new nonstate enterprises in the rural sector. Furthermore, it avoided financial problems by requiring those new enterprises to be self-financed. Equally important, China was able to introduce its reforms in an orderly fashion under a strong government that was capable of maintaining reasonable macroeconomic stability. An extraordinarily high level of private saving allowed it to cover its budget deficit and to continue giving large subsidies to the state-owned enterprises without having to resort to inflationary finance. In these respects, China provides a better example of a successful economic growth program than one of economic transition.

The reform of China's foreign trade regime has proceeded gradually, in a series of incremental changes since the mid-1980s, necessitated by the partial nature of the domestic price liberalization. The result has been an extremely rapid expansion of China's trade with the rest of the world, but also a complex and distortionary trade regime that may be more of a hindrance than a boon to China's future economic relations. At present, China's trade relations are quite shallow, as they consist largely of the reprocessing of imported materials for reexport. Here, too, it had an advantage in that overseas Chinese, operating out of Hong Kong, were willing to act as its agents in developing foreign markets. It has attracted substantial amounts of foreign finance, but more as a result of the investment opportunities that it created than because of any special official Western program of financial assistance. The extent of foreign interaction with the Chinese domestic economy remains limited. The external reforms have been an important complement to the domestic reforms that moved China toward greater reliance on markets. China may find it more difficult to move toward deeper integration with the global economy, however, because this will cause greater conflicts with the internal political system. To avoid disputes with its trading partners, China must unify and simplify its current trade regime. It must also broaden its trade links and join GATT.

The economic transition began under more difficult conditions in Central Europe, and perhaps insuperable ones in the republics of the former Soviet Union. Whereas parts of Central Europe are beginning a process of economic recovery, the decline in output has yet to turn around in most of the countries of the former Soviet Union. Differences in initial conditions help to account for the variations in economic performance. Certainly, the existence of a private sector and the decentralization of state enterprises in Central Europe speeded up the supply response to price liberalization in comparison with the response in the Soviet republics. And a reasonable degree of macroeconomic stability seemed to be another precondition of successful reform. Many of the shaky countries found it difficult to maintain the discipline of domestic fiscal and monetary policies in the transition to a democratic government, with all of its associated pressures from different interest groups. Although price liberalization brought a sharp acceleration of inflation, Czechoslovakia, Hungary, and Poland were able to restore a reasonable degree of price stability in its aftermath. Of the countries in transition, these three provide the most promising signs of positive growth in the future. These same three have also experienced rapid growth in employment in new private enterprises—primarily retail trade and services—which has helped offset the declining employment in their large industrial state enterprises. The privatization of these large-scale enterprises has moved more slowly.

Russia and the other republics remain in considerably greater turmoil. A small exception is the three Baltic states, which, because of their initial conditions and progress toward implementing reform programs, are more appropriately grouped with the economies of Central Europe. Although Russia has now managed to curb inflation, it may be unable to sustain its macroeconomic policies because of the large budget deficit, the continuing financial deterioration of the major enterprises, and a high degree of monopolization that inhibits the restructuring on the supply side of the economy. Although markets have emerged in the former Soviet republics, many of these countries are still struggling to create a stable commercial environment in which growth can occur. The Mafia and the breakdown of laws governing commercial activities, in particular, have kept the private sector from expanding.

The collapse of CMEA and interrepublic trade contributed to sharp reductions in output after 1990. This is another complicating factor in the European transition programs that was not present for China. Between 1989 and 1992 exports of the three major Central European economies (Czechoslovakia, Hungary, and Poland) to other CMEA countries declined by an estimated 50 percent. Russia's reported trade (exports plus imports) with CMEA countries outside the former Soviet Union fell from $66 billion in 1990 to $13 billion in 1992. Its trade with the other republics is reported to have dropped by at least 50 percent.

In contrast to China, the major economies of Central Europe acted quickly to eliminate the state monopoly over external trade and to establish most of the conditions for current account convertibility with low levels of tariff protection. The faster pace of reform was also consistent with their decision to implement domestic price liberalization more quickly and completely than China. As small economies, they opted for an outward-oriented reform program that used the global market as a guide in establishing a new domestic price structure and in defining comparative advantage. What has emerged is a simpler, more transparent trade regime, similar to that of Western Europe.

Most Western governments responded to the new situation by revising their trade rules so as to provide the transitional economies with access to global markets that is on a par with that enjoyed by the developing economies. The European Union and EFTA went further and signed association agreements with the countries of Central Europe that provide more favored trade relations by reducing tariffs below the levels that apply to other countries. Complaints about the association agreements relate primarily to the fact that they stop well short of providing these countries with trade status equivalent to membership in the economic union. The agreements include special provisions for several sensitive sectors in which the transitional economies have significant export potential, but in which the union is plagued with excess capacity. These special provisions (which apply to agricultural products, apparel, iron and steel, and chemicals) are estimated to cover as much as half of Central European exports to the European Union.

For Central Europe, the initial response of trade with the West was highly favorable, but only with extremely low real exchange rates that made exports extraordinarily cheap in Western markets. Exports to the industrial countries doubled between 1989 and 1992. The growth of trade has been heavily oriented toward Western Europe, and Germany has quickly emerged as the most important trading partner for nearly all of the Eastern and Central European countries. The rise of real exchange rates after 1992 and the correction of some of the most extreme imbalances of demand and supply in the domestic market weakened some of these export incentives, and growing balance of payments restraints have required some backpedaling on the initial commitment to liberal trade policies.

The economies of Central Europe have been unable to finance significant current account deficits: private capital inflows have amounted to a few billion dollars a year, and official assistance has been heavily concentrated in the refinancing of old debts that would not have been repaid in the absence of concessions. Contrary to some initial expectations, the rebuilding of the transitional economies has, to date, represented a trivial claim on international capital markets.

The reform of the trade sector within the former Soviet Union has been more chaotic. Many of the initial problems were greatly complicated by a collapse in the value of the ruble that created extreme divergences between the domestic and world market prices of basic commodities. Exports of these commodities also became an important mechanism for capital flight. The government was pressured to use large amounts of its foreign exchange earnings to subsidize the imports of basic commodities that had suddenly become prohibitively expensive in the domestic currency.

Dissolution of the Soviet Union created further problems for inter-republic trade. Initially, the new republics tried to maintain a monetary union based on the ruble, but without the discipline of a single central monetary authority. Efforts by Russia to impose discipline and reduce the flow of subsidies to the other states led them to introduce their own currencies; but the region lacked any payments system to finance trade among the states. Thus, they have been forced back to a system of more managed state trade. They have not been able to establish current account convertibility among themselves or with the external world economy.

The large size of the internal economy and abundant natural resources of Russia seem to call for external trade policies that are quite different from the strategies adopted by the small states of Central Europe. Although the ultimate goal should be to become part of the global economy, there is some justification for maintaining a temporary system of protective tariffs in Russia. Such a system would give Russian industry time to achieve a degree of restructuring that would allow it to compete with foreign manufactured products within the domestic economy. This structure of moderate tariffs should decline over time at a predetermined rate, and it should not apply to financial and other services where there is no existing capability. Furthermore, the difficulties faced by the other republics suggest that they should put maximum emphasis in the immediate future on building free-market trade links with Russia.

The three groups of countries discussed in this volume also differ in their prospects for achieving sustained economic growth and further integration into the global economy. China has been enormously successful in achieving rapid growth and in implementing a program of shallow integration with the global economy. But deeper integration with the global system may not be possible because of the incomplete nature of the reforms.

In contrast, the major Central European countries have jumped ahead of China in implementing the institutional aspects of current account convertibility. Whether they can catch up and become integrated with the economies of Western Europe will depend primarily on developments within the domestic economy. The transition is almost over, and they need to adopt domestic programs that emphasize growth. In this respect, they lag behind China. They have not been able to generate the high levels of domestic saving and incentives for investment in modern technologies that are needed to promote rapid growth. On the external side, the central issue is how far and how fast they can integrate with the European Union. It will be difficult for them to move beyond association status to full membership, unless the current union agrees to alter some of its institutions, such as the Common Agricultural Policy. This would require a significant change of direction for the European Union, away from deep political and economic union among a small number of similar countries toward a looser confederation. Such issues remain highly controversial and suggest that full membership lies well in the future.

The outlook for Russia and the other republics is extremely uncertain. They have not yet managed to build the institutional framework of a market economy, and many of them have only thin political support for reform. Nor have they progressed as far as China or Central Europe in establishing a functioning foreign trade regime and expanding their trade relations with the global economy. Even at a shallow level of trade in goods, their integration with the global economy remains limited. Here, too, most of the barriers to deeper integration with the global economy are domestic in origin.

The implications for the transitional economies of recent efforts among the industrial countries to move beyond the traditional emphasis on trade in goods and enact an agenda of measures involving deeper economic integration are mixed. The transitional countries are still struggling to establish the institutions required for reasonably efficient trade, and they are very much in the middle of a process of developing new areas of comparative advantage. On the positive side, they should benefit from the expansion of trade in business and financial services because their own activities in these areas remain far behind those of the West. They would gain from importing the greater expertise and efficiency of Western financial institutions. Since they are only now establishing rules governing competition and commercial practices, they also have an opportunity to avoid some of the transitional costs that others will encounter in harmonizing their commercial regulations with global practices. They can use the emerging international commercial standards as the guide for their own.

On the other hand, with only a few exceptions, services are not likely to be areas of comparative advantage for these countries. New rules governing the protection of intellectual property rights may also raise the cost of adopting new technologies. Most important, it will be many years before their domestic financial markets will develop the degree of resiliency required to allow the free flow of financial capital. Pressures to open up their financial markets at the same pace with which they sought integration with international markets in goods and services may introduce risks of economic instability, similar to those that have plagued Latin America.

Comments

Alan Gelb

This volume does not approach integration in a narrow sense but offers a broad and, on the whole, balanced and pragmatic assessment of experience across a wide range of countries: the still chaotic former Soviet Union; growing, gradualist China; and the radical reformers in Eastern Europe, which now seem to be on the way to recovery. Although there are still many unknowns (for example, how best to cope with poverty or bad debts in transition), some patterns are clearer than they were a year ago. The experience of Ukraine and other countries disposes of the thought that "nonreform" is a viable option for countries caught within the rubble of the Soviet system. It also casts doubt on the feasibility of gradualism for such countries. Radical reform, though still historically unprecedented, has begun to acquire some sort of track record to aid assessment. Although the picture is far from rosy, some of the countries have surmounted the "first-stage" problems of stabilization and liberalization and are well into grappling with such "second-stage" issues as bad debts, unemployment, and poverty. We also understand better than before some of the reasons for the different response of China and Vietnam to reforms. The book provides a useful comparative discussion of such issues.

As the volume argues, integration of the formerly centrally planned economies (the term *transitional economies* will be used below) is an

Alan Gelb is chief of the Transition Economics Division at the World Bank.

155

extremely critical component of their reforms. Integration has several levels: goods and nonfactor services markets; capital flows, direct foreign investment, and skills transfer; the creation of legal, regulatory, and social institutions that conform to global norms; and the reorganization of information flows that were previously hierarchical and controlled. In all these dimensions, the economic and political heritage of the transitional economies is one of autarky. Opening up is a prerequisite for these economies to acquire the skills and institutions needed to become truly competitive in the global economy. Indeed what is really distinctive about the transitional economy reform problem (especially for transitional economies in Eastern Europe and the former Soviet Union) is the combination of such deep autarky with highly sophisticated technical skills. Neither developed nor developing economies, they are unbalanced by market economy standards: long on industrial production but short on quality control, marketing, financial, and other services.

At the same time, the larger economies—China and particularly Russia—are far from *internally* integrated economies. China still places formal constraints on labor mobility; though weakening, these account for part of the high rural-urban differentials and increasing regional disparities observed in that country. There are also constraints on the internal capital mobility and on interprovincial trade. Although residential controls may have been lifted in Russia, there are still considerable barriers to internal integration, involving the monopolization of large-scale trade, storage, and distribution networks; regulatory inconsistencies; and local price controls. As shown by recent research on patterns of agricultural price formation, the latter still have an impact on the spatial distribution of prices.

The Liberalization-Stabilization Link

As noted in the text, governments cannot easily impose hard budget constraints on enterprises unless markets are allowed to function. This link between liberalization and stabilization has emerged as one of the most robust cross-country relationships for Eastern Europe and the former Soviet Union.[1] Governments that have not

1. See De Melo, Denizer, and Gelb (forthcoming b).

liberalized extensively have typically continued to support their industrial and farming sectors with large doses of directed credit, adding to quasi-fiscal deficits and prolonging high inflation long after the initial burst when prices were freed. For some of the slow reformers, quasi-fiscal subsidies have represented on the order of 20 percent of gross domestic product (GDP). The question of how fast markets should be liberalized is therefore as much a *macro* question as a *micro* one for these countries, and although liberalization brings its own tendencies toward macrodestabilization, on balance it seems that macro arguments press for more rapid, rather than gradual, liberalization. It is tempting to use price controls to cushion adjustment stresses, and under some circumstances (for example, energy prices and rents in the Czech Republic) this may be done without disrupting macroeconomic balance.

In China, on the other hand, macroeconomic instability has followed the failure of fiscal and monetary policies to keep abreast of the progressive liberalization of goods and financial markets, and the growth of competition that has undercut the state sector. On a deeper level, many of China's reform problems noted in the text are related to a central issue: the indeterminacy of property rights in China and the consequent socialization of risk, at least for the state sector. This contributes to a chronic excess demand, particularly for investment goods, and to a three-level game—between enterprises, subnational government, and central government—that has weakened macro control.

Microeconomic Arguments for Protection

Despite the macro argument, should there be temporary selective protection to allow firms time to adjust to international competition? I agree that the comparative advantage of Russia and some other states of the former Soviet Union in mineral resources may call for manufacturing to be protected for an extended period to aid adjustment, or as a (suboptimal) way of distributing mineral rent across the population. But it is more difficult to make the case for other countries. By and large, Eastern Europe must depend on industrial exports for hard currency, and it has been far more successful in this area than most would have predicted a few years ago. With reappreciation of real exchange rates toward levels roughly as predicted by purchasing power parity (PPP) theory, there has been some retreat from initially very open trade toward rising and differentiated tariffs. This may be undesirable; given political realities, perhaps it is unavoidable. Membership in the General Agreement on Tariffs and Trade and the World Trade Organization seems to be potentially important, serving as it does to limit the tendency for other countries to impose barriers to trade among themselves. But if a rapid move toward free trade is endorsed for Eastern Europe, how does this bear on the assessment of China's relatively slow and selective trade transition, involving, in particular, extended protection of consumer goods industries? More comparative discussion of this question would be welcome.

Access to world markets is vitally important for transitional countries. Although there has been progress, restraints on sensitive industrial sectors are estimated to affect directly one third of their capacity, and they face competition from subsidized producers, especially in agriculture. Does the existence of the Common Agricultural Policy provide a valid argument for agricultural protection in Eastern Europe? My own view is probably not, but there are various opinions on this question. Energy is another area in which import restrictions in industrial countries pose a potential barrier to moving toward world prices within the transitional countries—the former Soviet Union has the potential to generate an enormous natural gas surplus but confronts oligopolistic utilities in the West as well as pipeline transit problems. Without greatly increased export opportunities, it is likely that gas prices will remain far below world levels in much of the former Soviet Union, with implications for the global competitiveness of important energy-intensive sectors.

Real Exchange Rates through Transition

At the start of reforms, real exchange rates were very heavily depreciated, but the experience of countries that have managed to restore macroeconomic stability, including the leading reformers in Eastern Europe, suggests that they reappreciate to the range of 50 percent of their estimated PPP level. Comparative analysis suggests that this is actually not out of line with the average ratio between PPP and market exchange rates for countries at about the same level of PPP income per head. Countries that have not managed to stabilize experience prolonged depreciation resulting from capital flight. Second-generation stabilizers in the midst of programs, such as Romania and Armenia, are also seeing a firming of their real exchange rates, and this is needed to enable markets to work competitively.

From such a perspective, a Russian rate set at one-third of PPP, cited in the text, is not so far out of a medium-run equilibrium as might be thought. In the absence of a fairy godmother, export growth (and in some cases return of flight capital) must be the main motor for the recovery and growth of the transitional economies, as it usually has been for other countries experiencing a turnaround.

It should be noted that the combination of a still-open trade policy (even with higher tariffs) and a firming exchange rate has indeed placed firms under considerable competitive pressure. Surveys of firms in Poland show that in many cases their main competition after 1991 has been perceived to be imports rather than other domestic firms. Surveys of Russian firms have also suggested a surprising degree of competition in view of the supposedly monopolistic nature of industry, and an appreciable impact of imports for many. Firm-level studies for Eastern Europe and the former Soviet Union cannot easily separate the effects of competition from many other influences, but studies for China support the proposition that productivity gains have indeed been largest in the state enterprises most exposed to market forces, where such gains are measured by the shares of their outputs and inputs traded outside the plan and also by the share of competitive nonstate industry in the same province.

The persistence of an unusually large divergence between market and PPP exchange rates for China is puzzling. China's opening has caused its exchange rate to devalue in real terms, and the result has been a sharp widening of the gap between PPP and exchange-rate-based levels of income, to the point where the former China's reported dollar GDP per head was declining steadily, over a period during which it had reportedly one of the highest growth rates in the world. (This fact has not gone unnoticed by critics of World Bank data.) It is generally agreed that China's economy is far larger, in dollars, than it would appear from exchange conversion data; estimates of trade ratios to GDP are therefore seriously biased.[2]

2. See, for example, Gelb, Jefferson, and Singh (1993) and references cited therein.

Payment and Related Problems

The book's suggestion that the breakdown of trade within the former Soviet Union has been more costly than suboptimal external trade is surely correct. A large part of the problem involves the breakdown of payments mechanisms. Not only have monetary arrangements in much of the former Soviet Union been in chaos, but banks and other financial institutions lack the creditworthiness, and in some cases the capacity and resources, to finance trade effectively. In most of the countries, strengthening financial institutions to facilitate trade is probably a more urgent priority than developing their capacity to fund investments, and the transitional countries are now disadvantaged, relative to industrial countries, in this area. Foreign involvement combining financial assistance (or guarantees to selected banks) and technical assistance can play a bridging role. Innovative programs may support trade without necessarily going through banks at all, in countries where banks are judged unable to evaluate and bear commercial risk. For example, one World Bank project is being developed for Moldova to cover political and policy risk, with the aim of attracting financing for preexport transactions (such as the supply of key imported inputs) from traders, foreign suppliers, and buyers. This approach will allow a wider range of screening for commercial risk. Such measures, though not comprehensive solutions, can make a useful contribution. Creation of a foreign exchange pool to facilitate hard-currency clearing will be problematic unless policies to encourage domestic savings and the return of flight capital are far stronger than they have been.

Legal Reform and Harmonization

Finally, it is perhaps surprising that a book so sensitive to the importance of institutional development does not discuss more extensively the integration issues that arise in this sphere. Should the countries of Eastern Europe (and the former Soviet Union) transplant European Union models, or must they build on their own legal heritage, which was interrupted by communist takeover? How appropriate is the German model of regulatory transplantation, and how transferrable? To what extent is deep integration of China's economy possible, without thorough reform (or development) of the legal underpinnings of its market economy? Although interest in China continues unabated, there are signs that the weakness of the legal framework is inhibiting the involvement of large-scale corporate investors.

Conclusion

At the level of market products, the process of integrating formerly planned economies into the global economy has come a long way, more rapidly than might have been predicted ten years ago. More remains to be done, however, particularly in widening the scope of foreign investment activities and in reshaping institutions in many reforming countries to meet world standards.

Richard Portes

This is a comprehensive study that goes well beyond an analysis of economic integration to consider the entire process of economic transformation from socialist central planning to a capitalist market economy. It is also far reaching geographically: it covers the countries of Central and Eastern Europe, the former Soviet Union, and China—only Vietnam and Mongolia appear to have been left out. So although I am broadly sympathetic to the book's approach and many of its conclusions, there are still many qualifications to add and questions to raise, and even some disagreements to register.

The Strategy of Economic Transformation

The authors are wise not to base their analysis on "shock versus gradualism," nor to go very far in characterizing policy differences in these terms. But that view of the issues does occasionally creep into the argument, and it only misleads. It is not helpful to dispute whether Russia actually tried shock therapy, whether Polish radicalism has been more successful than Hungarian gradualism, or whether Chinese gradualism is inapplicable to Eastern Europe because of different initial conditions. There can be no single preferred strategy independent of initial conditions, nor does any actual policy path fit any simple model very well.

A more helpful version of this debate concerns the sequencing of policies in their implementation. The opening package of measures must be sufficient to make the regime change credible, but it is administratively impossible and economically unwise to try to do everything at once. The legal, institutional, economic, and behavioral infrastructure of the capitalist market economy could only be installed quickly by a government as authoritarian as the worst of those overthrown in the revolutions of 1989 (or in the exceptional circumstances of Germany). Thus policymakers *must* choose a sequence. Insofar as possible, they should do so consciously rather than merely follow the political winds.

This position may well be gradualism, but that term is widely misinterpreted: a gradualist program for a sequence of policy mea-

Richard Portes is professor of economics at the London Business School and director of the Centre for Economic Policy Research.

sures is just the opposite of the uncoordinated improvisation of which gradualism is often accused; if it really is drift, then it is not deliberate policy. On the other hand, avoiding drift in a gradualist program does require some ability to precommit, as well as to retain credibility when political imperatives or exogenous shocks force reoptimization. That is hard, so trying to do everything at once may actually seem easier. It is not, nor is it feasible.[1]

We should therefore beware of those who take the conventional refuge of the ideologue in claiming that the (shock therapy) program has not failed, instead that it has just not been implemented fully and consistently. That is a hypothesis that is in principle not testable, because it will always be possible to find a "key" element of the program that could not be applied.

In any case, there is usually little margin for choice. Some elements of stabilization and liberalization make sense only when carried out simultaneously. The range observed across countries is in fact surprisingly limited and mainly a function of initial conditions. Foresight, sequencing, implementation, and political support are the key differences and potential weaknesses. And no country fits particularly well the stereotype that the ideologues assign to it: "gradualist" Hungary was much more "radical" than Poland in its implementation of bankruptcy legislation, and Czechoslovakia was more "radical" than either with its voucher privatization program.

The choices posed by sequencing are not merely sources of academic dispute. There are serious decisions to be made, for example, about the priority to be given to privatization of large state-owned enterprises relative to other institutional changes and demonopolization, and about the urgency of creating a healthy structure of financial intermediation.

The broadest and most important of these issues is the relative priority given to macroeconomic and microeconomic policies. I have argued that a major error in the strategy of transformation, repeated in many countries, was the overemphasis on macroeconomic policy and the view that macroeconomic stabilization was a precondition for success in all the other dimensions of transformation.[2] The authors unfortunately appear to share that view, despite contrary evidence

1. See the excellent discussion in European Bank for Reconstruction and Development (1994b, chap. 3).
2. Portes (1991c, 1994b, 1994c).

from Latin America and from the sweeping privatization in macroeconomically unstable Russia.[3]

Political capital depreciates rapidly; administrative resources are limited. Both should be allocated to their most productive uses. In Russia at the beginning of 1992, for example, macroeconomic stabilization was bound to fail, whatever the volume of Western aid (within feasible limits). Therefore the priorities should have been the energy sector, agriculture, and housing.[4] The preoccupation with stabilization is partly a reflection of the leading role of the International Monetary Fund (IMF) and its macroeconomic conditionality, which in turn is a key element of the "Washington consensus." That is not the fault of the Fund, which rightly focuses on short-run macroeconomic policies, but rather of the consensus strategy itself.

Domestic Policies

The main focus of the book is on external policies and integration, but a few key points in the authors' treatment of domestic policies require comment. Although they do acknowledge that the widespread, deep, and persistent fall in output in the transforming economies (except China) has been real rather than a statistical artifact, they line up with the current conventional wisdom that this fall was inevitable. Indeed they share the view that macroeconomic stabilization is always accompanied by a fall in output.

There are numerous counterexamples, however, of exchange-rate-based stabilizations followed by immediate production increases— that is indeed the normal outcome until appreciation of the real exchange rate starts to drag output down.[5] Why did none of those who now claim that a prolonged depression was inevitable warn all of us—and especially the population in the countries of Central and Eastern Europe and the former Soviet Union—in the winter of 1989– 90, or at least by 1991? The answer is that many of those now making this claim were (and still are) advocates of or responsible for the policy errors that were in good part at fault. As Rosati puts it, "To summarize, the output fall in the first stage of transition . . . was to a

3. For the Latin American evidence, see Edwards (1994).
4. Portes (1992b).
5. Végh (1991).

large extent a result of a combination of *excessive* demand cuts and policy-induced supply shocks" (emphasis in original).[6]

I have argued that there were key errors and omissions in both macro- and microeconomic policies, but that the latter were more important. In particular, there was inadequate emphasis—as there is in this study—on creating a functioning system of financial intermediation, especially on making it possible for the banks to operate effectively.[7] Moreover, the stress on rapid privatization (which proved hard to implement) ignored the opportunities for improving the performance of the large state-owned enterprises.[8] At the very least, these factors are the primary causes of the depth and duration of the depression following the initial shocks.

We must certainly reject the authors' broad assertion that the comparable size of the decline in output across the countries of Central and Eastern Europe shows that policies could not have played a significant role. Economists are accustomed to modeling outcomes as the consequences of multiple causes, a process in which the weights may be the same across observations, whereas the sizes of individual influences may differ. Policies did differ across countries; so did initial conditions. For example, Hungary did not devalue excessively but had a heavy debt service burden, mishandled its banking sector, and implemented crude, draconian bankruptcy policies. Poland devalued excessively and implemented a credit crunch, but obtained debt relief. Why should these differences imply that policies did not affect the outcomes significantly? One may also query the authors' uncritical acceptance of the view that these economies had overbuilt heavy industries and that significant amounts of their output were not marketable under the new conditions. In fact, the countries of Central and Eastern Europe did increase their exports of manufactures (Standard International Trade Classification categories 6–8) to the European Union (EU) very rapidly—on the order of 25 percent per annum—during the period 1989–93. Winters's detailed analysis of steel (the archetypal "overbuilt heavy industry") argues against any rapid, substantial contraction.[9]

6. Rosati (1994, p. 435).
7. Portes (1991c, 1993b); Begg and Portes (1993).
8. Grosfeld and Roland (1995).
9. See Faini and Portes (1995, pp. 3–5, 230–31).

External Policies

On exchange rate policy and convertibility, I broadly endorse the authors' views. From the outset, I have argued for early current account convertibility wherever this is feasible without excessive exchange rate depreciation. Capital account convertibility, on the other hand, has clear dangers[10]—Mexico is not the only "emerging market" in which serious instability is possible, even likely.

The authors do not consider the extreme option of the currency board.[11] I believe that the claims made on behalf of this policy are exaggerated—indeed, the case for Estonia as a triumph both of the currency board and of IMF policies (never mind the Fund's initial opposition!) seems somewhat overstated in view of the bank failures and deep fall in output there. A currency board eliminates the lender of last resort, offers no alternative protection against systemic financial risk, and can easily lead to overvaluation.

The book argues in the context of Russia for the use of tariff protection in the initial stages of transition. The case is strong, and it could have applied to Eastern Europe as well, at least until those countries constrained themselves in the Europe Agreements with the EU.[12] Tariffs would have offered revenue, interim protection for "senile" industries, and less need for exchange rate protection, that is, excessive devaluation. The initial devaluations overshot, partly because all forms of protection were removed simultaneously.[13] Subsequently there has been a natural process of real exchange rate appreciation, while domestic political pressures have brought back protection, as one would have expected.[14] A more gradual process of reducing protection, with the backing of conditionality associated with agreements with the EU, could have been more unidirectional and robust.

The authors do not make any judgments on the long-run comparative advantage and likely trade patterns of the countries of Central

10. Portes (1991b, 1994a).
11. As proposed for the countries of the former Soviet Union by Hanke, Jonung, and Schuler (1993).
12. See also Aghion and others (1992); European Bank for Reconstruction and Development (1994b); Portes (1994b).
13. See the chapter by Summers in Blejer and others (1993), which criticizes the abrupt elimination of protection in Poland.
14. Halpern and Wyplosz (forthcoming); Winters (1995).

and Eastern Europe. Perhaps this is because the substantial literature on these issues is somewhat contradictory.[15] Nevertheless, this is a key issue for intra-EU decisionmaking regarding policies toward the countries of Central and Eastern Europe, as well as for their long-run position vis-à-vis the East Asian countries. Any discussion of these countries' economic integration with the international economy should take a position on this point.

Economic Integration

The issues here are quite different between the countries of Central and Eastern Europe, the former Soviet Union, and China. For most of the countries of Central and Eastern Europe, there is a realistic prospect of joining the EU in the foreseeable future. Although intraregional integration is a serious issue for them as well, it is much more important for the countries of the former Soviet Union. For China, the main issues are the speed and modalities of opening the economy to trade and foreign investment.

A payments union was never a serious prospect, either among the countries of Central and Eastern Europe and the former Soviet Union, or among the latter alone; even the Interstate Bank for the former Soviet Union was a chimera. On the other hand, the East Europeans were mistaken to rush headlong into the deliberate destruction of the Council for Mutual Economic Assistance institutional framework for their trade. But this is history; the best that can be done now is to work toward more intraregional cooperation.[16]

For these countries, the steps toward economic integration with the rest of the world are uneven and difficult. Merely joining the General Agreement on Tariffs and Trade/World Trade Organization is proving a complex problem for China, already involving significant adaptation of its internal legal and economic institutions. Most of the former Soviet Union can look forward to something like free trade agreements with the EU in manufactures, with transition periods. These too will require adaptation, but perhaps as much by the EU as by those countries entering preferential trade agreements with it.

15. See, for example, Hamilton and Winters (1992); Neven (forthcoming).
16. Baldwin (1994); Nuti and Portes (1993).

Already much deeper and more ambitious are the Europe Agreements between the EU and six of the countries of Central and Eastern Europe (soon to be nine, with the Baltic countries, and then ten, with Slovenia).[17] That is so not just because these are now explicitly meant to lead to accession to the EU in due course (though with no specific time frame). Rather the key aspect of these accords is that they do envisage deep integration in certain dimensions. In particular, the "approximation of laws" accepted by the East Europeans, including adoption of EU competition policies, implies a wide-ranging adaptation of these economies to EU legal standards and institutions, with serious constraints on behavior.[18] It might have been easier if from the outset the market economy in the East had been constructed so as to be compatible with EU laws and institutions, and this might have been a useful constraint on domestic politics and politicians.[19] The commitment has now been accepted, but it will be difficult to implement, even when the EU sets out clearly the requirements that the internal market will impose on the aspirant countries.

EU membership itself will go well beyond the single European market. It is a bigger step than the countries of Central and Eastern Europe themselves realize, substantially bigger than that taken by Spain and Portugal at the time of their accession.[20] It includes not just harmonization of laws and standards but adoption of EU policies on such matters as state aids, environmental standards, and social policies, and opening up to competition from the EU, not just in industry but also in financial and other services. There are also the Common Agricultural Policy, migration, and the Maastricht provisions for economic and monetary union. The problems that these pose for the EU are widely understood in the West—especially the budgetary implications.[21] However, the countries of Central and Eastern Europe have not yet seriously begun to come to grips with the process of deep integration and its implications. They may discover it is all rather more difficult than they expected.

17. Portes (1992a).
18. Hoekman and Mavroidis (forthcoming); Sapir (1995).
19. Portes (1991c).
20. See Baldwin (1994).
21. As Baldwin (1994) has put it, under current policies these countries are too poor, too agricultural, and too populous to join the EU.

I would have liked to see this book give a much more extensive treatment of the preconditions for deep integration: How developed and how strong must domestic markets and institutions be to withstand the shocks of opening up fully? What dangers are there in prematurely embracing institutional as well as economic competition from abroad? How do the particular history and characteristics of the economies exiting from socialist central planning affect their readiness for deep integration and the path they will have to follow to achieve it?

Finally, I regret that the authors did not devote any attention to the relations between the transforming countries and international institutions. The issues here include not merely the influence of those institutions on the policies of the countries of Central and Eastern Europe, the former Soviet Union, and China, but also how bringing these countries into the system and dealing with them is likely to affect the institutions themselves.[22] In this respect as in others, deep integration is a reciprocal process. Helping the transforming economies has put strains on the IMF and the World Bank, both internally and in their relations with the G-7 and its most powerful members. It has also exposed failures of coordination, going as far as battles for turf among the international institutions themselves (including not just the Fund and the Bank, but also the European Bank for Reconstruction and Development, the Organization for Economic Cooperation and Development, the European Commission, the Export-Import Bank, and others). A Washington-based but detached view of these problems would have been very useful, partly as a reflection on a key feature of the long-run deep integration process, and partly in view of the short- and medium-run reconsideration of roles of the international institutions launched by the G-7 in 1994.

22. See Gomulka (forthcoming); Portes (1994c).

References

Aghion, Philippe, R. Burgess, Jean-Paul Fitoussi, and Patrick A. Messerlin. 1992. "Towards a European Continental Common Market." London: European Bank for Reconstruction and Development.

Anderson, Kym. 1990. "China's Economic Growth, Changing Competitive Advantages and Agricultural Trade." *Review of Marketing and Agricultural Economics* 58 (April): 56–75.

Aslund, Anders. 1993. "The Nature of the Transformation Crisis in the Former Soviet Countries." Stockholm School of Economics.

Baldwin, Richard E. 1994. *Toward an Integrated Europe.* London: Centre for Economic Policy Research.

Beenstock, Michael. 1992. "The Reintegration of Eastern Europe into the World Economy." Hebrew University Working Paper 254. Jerusalem.

Begg, David, and Richard Portes. 1993. "Enterprise Debt and Economic Transformation: Financial Restructuring of the State Sector in Central and Eastern Europe." In *Capital Markets and Financial Intermediation,* edited by Colin Mayer and Xavier Vives, 230–55. Cambridge University Press.

Belkindas, Misha, and Yuri Dikhanov. 1994. "Foreign Trade Statitistics in the Former Soviet Union." In *Trade in the New Independent States,* edited by Constantine Michalopoulos and David Tarr, 21–28. Washington: World Bank.

Bell, Michael W., Hoe Ee Khor, and Kalpana Kochhar. 1993. "China at the Threshold of a Market Economy." IMF Occasional Paper 107. Washington.

Blanchard, Olivier, Simon Commander, and Fabrizio Coricelli. 1995. "Unemployment and Restructuring in Eastern Europe and Russia." In *Unemployment, Restructuring and the Labor Market in Eastern Europe and Russia,* edited by Commander and Coricelli, 289–329. Washington: World Bank.

Blanchard, Olivier, and others. 1991. *Reform in Eastern Europe.* MIT Press.

Blejer, Mario I. 1993. "Gaidar's Economic Reforms Were Not a Failure: Some Reflections on Russia's Economic Performance in 1992." Washington: World Bank.

Blejer, Mario I., and others. 1991. "China: Economic Reform and Macroeconomic Management." IMF Occasional Paper 76. Washington.

171

————, eds. 1993. *Eastern Europe in Transition: From Recession to Growth.* Washington: World Bank.

Bofinger, Peter. 1991. "Options for the Payments and Exchange-Rate System in Eastern Europe." *European Economy.* Special edition 2: *The Path of Reform in Central and Eastern Europe,* 243–62.

Bofinger, Peter, and Daniel Gross. 1992. "A Multilateral Payments Union for the Commonwealth of Independent States: Why and How?" Centre for Economic Policy Research Discussion Paper 654. London.

Borensztein, Eduardo, Dimitri Demekas, and Jonathan Ostry. 1993. "An Empirical Analysis of the Output Decline in Three Eastern European Countries." *IMF Staff Papers* 40 (March): 1–31.

Boycko, Maxim, Andrei Shleifer, and Robert Vishny. 1993. "Privatizing Russia." *Brookings Papers on Economic Activity* 2: 139–92.

Brada, Josef C. 1993. "The Transformation from Communism to Capitalism: How Far? How Fast?" *Post-Soviet Affairs* 9 (April-June): 87–110.

Brown, Annette N., Barry Ickes, and Randy Ryterman. 1993. "The Myth of Monopoly: A New View of Industrial Structure in Russia." Working Paper 10-5-93 (August). Department of Economics, Pennsylvania State University.

Brown, Stuart, and Misha Belkindas. 1993. "Who's Feeding Whom? An Analysis of Soviet Interrepublic Trade." In *The Former Soviet Union in Transition,* U.S. Congress, Joint Economic Committee. Washington: U.S. Government Printing Office.

Bruno, Michael. 1992. "Stabilization and Reform in Eastern Europe: A Preliminary Analysis." *IMF Staff Papers* 39 (December): 741–77.

————. 1993. *Crisis, Stabilization and Economic Reform: Therapy by Consensus.* Clarendon Press.

Calvo, Guillermo, and Fabrizio Coricelli. 1993. "Output Collapse in Eastern Europe: The Role of Credit." *IMF Staff Papers* 40 (March): 32–52.

Centre for Economic Policy Research (CEPR). 1990. *Monitoring European Integration: The Impact of Eastern Europe.* London.

Chenery, Hollis B., and Moshe Syrquin. 1975. *Patterns of Development, 1950–1970.* Oxford University Press.

Christensen, Benedicte V. 1994. *The Russian Federation in Transition: External Developments.* IMF Occasional Paper 111. Washington.

Collins, Susan M., and Dani Rodrik. 1991. *Eastern Europe and the Soviet Union in the World Economy.* Washington: Institute for International Economics.

Connolly, Michael, and Silvina Vatnick. 1994. "Uzbekistan: Trade in a Cotton Based Economy." In *Trade in the New Independent States,* Studies of Economies in Transformation 13, edited by Constantine Michalopoulos and David G. Tarr, 199–210. Washington: World Bank.

De Melo, Martha, Cevdet Denizer, and Alan Gelb. Forthcoming, a. "The Macroeconomic Context of Transition." Washington: World Bank.

————. Forthcoming, b. "Patterns and Progress of Transition." Policy Research Department Report. Washington: World Bank.

Dyker, David. 1993a. "Free Trade and Fair Trade with Eastern Europe." *RFE/RL Research Report* 2 (June 25): 39–42.

———. 1993b. "Russian Perceptions of Economic Security." London: Royal Institute of International Affairs.

Easterly, William, and Paulo Viera da Cunha. 1994. "Financing the Storm: Macroeconomic Crisis in Russia." Washington: World Bank.

Easterly, William, and Stanley Fischer. 1993. "The Soviet Economic Decline: Historical and Republican Data." MIT Press.

Edwards, Sebastian. 1994. "Macroeconomic Stabilization in Latin America: Recent Experience and Some Sequencing Issues." National Bureau of Economic Research Working Paper 4697. Cambridge, Mass.

European Bank for Reconstruction and Development (EBRD). 1993. *EBRD Economic Review: Current Economic Issues.* London (July).

———. 1994a. *Economics of Transition* 2 (March): 118–27.

———. 1994b. *Transition Report.* London (July).

Faini, Riccardo, and Richard Portes, eds. 1995. *European Union Trade with Eastern Europe: Adjustment and Opportunities.* London: Centre for Economic Policy Research.

Fischer, Stanley. 1993. "Economic Performance in the FSU, Mid-1993." Cambridge, Mass.: Department of Economics, Massachusetts Institute of Technology.

Fischer, Stanley, and Alan Gelb. 1991. "The Process of Socialist Economic Transformation." *Journal of Economic Perspectives* 5 (Fall): 91–105.

Fries, Stephen M., and Timothy D. Lane. 1994. "Financial and Enterprise Restructuring in Emerging Market Economies." In *Building Sound Finance in Emerging Market Economies,* edited by Gerard Caprio, David Folkerts-Landau, and Timothy D. Lane, 21–46. Washington: International Monetary Fund.

Gelb, Alan, Gary Jefferson, and Inderjit Singh. 1993. "Can Communist Countries Transform Incrementally? The Experience of China." *Economics of Transition* 1 (December): 401–35.

General Agreement on Tariffs and Trade. 1993. *International Trade 1993: Statistics.* Geneva.

Gomulka, Stanislaw. 1993. "Poland: Glass Half Full." In *Economic Transformation in Central Europe,* edited by Richard Portes, 211–73. London: Centre for Economic Policy Research.

———. Forthcoming. "The Role of International Financial Institutions: The Polish and Russian Experiences 1989–94." *Journal of Comparative Economics.*

Government of the Russian Federation. 1993. *Russian Economic Trends: Quarterly Report* 3. London: Whurr Publishers.

———. 1994a. *Russian Economic Trends: Monthly Update* (August). London: Whurr Publishers.

———. 1994b. *Russian Economic Trends: Monthly Update* (December). London: Whurr Publishers.

———. 1994c. *Russian Economic Trends: Quarterly Report* 2. London: Whurr Publishers.

Grosfeld, Irena, and Gérard Roland. 1995. "Enterprise Restructuring in Central Europe: What Remains to Be Done?" In *Economic Transformation: The Next Stage in Central Europe,* edited by Peter Bofinger and Richard Portes. London: Centre for Economic Policy Research.

Gulde, Anne Marie, and Marianne Schulze-Ghattas. 1993. "Purchasing Power Parity Based Weights for the *World Economic Outlook.*" In *Staff Studies for the World Economic Outlook* (December): 117.

Halpern, Laszlo, and Charles Wyplosz. Forthcoming. "Equilibrium Real Exchange Rates in Transition." In *Economic Transformation: The Next Stage in Central Europe,* edited by Peter Bofinger and Richard Portes. London: Centre for Economic Policy Research.

Hamilton, Carl, and L. Alan Winters. 1992. "Opening Up International Trade with Eastern Europe." *Economic Policy* 14 (April): 77–116.

Hanke, Steve H., Lars Jonung, and Kurt Schuler. 1993. *Russian Currency and Finance: A Currency Board Approach to Reform.* London: Routledge.

Hewett, Ed A., and Clifford Gaddy. 1992. *Open for Business: Russia's Return to the Global Economy.* Brookings.

Hindley, Brian. 1993. "Helping Transition through Trade? EC and US Policy towards Exports from Eastern and Central Europe." European Bank for Reconstruction and Development Working Paper 4 (March). London.

Hoekman, Bernard, and Petros Mavroidis. Forthcoming. "Linking Competition and Trade Policies in Central and East European Countries." In *Foundations of an Open Economy: Trade Laws and Institutions for Eastern Europe,* edited by L. Alan Winters. London: Centre for Economic Policy Research.

International Monetary Fund (IMF). 1991. *A Study of the Soviet Economy.* Washington.

———. 1993a. *Direction of Trade Statistics Yearbook 1986–92.* Washington.

———. 1993b. *Estonia.* IMF Economic Reviews 4 (May).

———. 1993c. *Latvia.* IMF Economic Reviews 6 (June).

———. 1993d. *Lithuania.* IMF Economic Reviews 7 (June).

———. 1993e. *Russian Federation.* IMF Economic Reviews 8 (June).

———. 1994a. *Balance of Payments Statistics Yearbook, 1994.* Washington.

———. 1994b. *Direction of Trade Statistics, 1987–93.* Washington.

———. 1994c. *International Financial Statistics* 47 (May). Washington.

———. 1994d. *International Financial Statistics Yearbook, 1993.* Washington.

———. 1994e. *World Economic Outlook* (May).

———. 1994f. *World Economic Outlook* (October).

Jefferson, Gary, Thomas Rawski, and Yuxin Zheng. 1992. "Growth, Efficiency, and Convergence in China's State and Collective Industry." *Economic Development and Cultural Change* 40:239–66.

Kenen, Peter. 1991. "Transitional Arrangements for Trade and Payments among the CMEA Countries." *IMF Staff Papers* 38 (June): 235–67.

Khor, Hoe Ee. 1993. "China's Foreign Currency Swap Market." IMF Paper on Policy Analysis and Assessment 94/1. Washington.

Kirmani, Nahhed, Klaus Enders, and Uwe Corsepius. 1994. "Trade Policy Reform in the Countries of the Former Soviet Union." *IMF Economic Review* 2 (February).

Konovalov, Vladimir. 1994. "Russian Trade Policy." In *Trade in the New Independent States,* Studies of Economies in Transformation 13, edited by Constantine Michalopoulos and David G. Tarr, 29–64. Washington: World Bank.

Lardy, Nicholas R. 1992. "Chinese Foreign Trade." *China Quarterly* 131 (September): 691–720.

———. 1994. *China in the World Economy.* Washington: Institute for International Economics.

Linder, Staffan. 1961. *An Essay on Trade and Transforation.* New York: John Wiley.

Litwack, John M. 1991. "Legality and Market Reform in Soviet-Type Economies." *Journal of Economic Perspectives* 5 (Fall): 77–90.

Markus, Ustina. 1994. "The Russian-Belarusian Monetary Union." *RFE/RL Research Report: 1993: The Year in Review* 3 (January): 28–32.

McGuckin, Robert H., and Sang V. Nguyen. 1993. "Post-Reform Industrial Productivity Performance of China: New Evidence from the 1985 Industrial Census Data." *Economic Inquiry* 31 (July): 323–41.

McKinnon, Ronald I. 1991. *The Order of Economic Liberalization: Financial Control in the Transition to a Market Economy.* Johns Hopkins University Press.

———. 1993a. "Macroeconomic Control in Liberalizing Socialist Economies: Asian and European Parallels." In *Finance and Development: Issues and Experience,* edited by Alberto Giovannini, 223–56. Cambridge University Press.

———. 1993b. "Gradual versus Rapid Liberalization in Socialist Economies: Financial Policies and Macroeconomic Stability in China and Russia Compared." Paper presented at the annual World Bank Conference on Development Economics, May 3–4, Washington.

McMillan, John, and Barry Naughton. 1992. "How to Reform a Planned Economy: Lessons from China." *Oxford Review of Economic Policy* 8 (1): 130–43.

Michaely, Michael, Demetrios Papageorgiou, and Armeane M. Choksi, eds. 1991. *Liberalizing Foreign Trade.* Vol. 7: *Lessons of Experience in the Developing World.* Cambridge, Mass.: Basil Blackwell.

Michalopoulos, Constantine, and David G. Tarr. 1994. "Summary and Overview of Developments since Independence." In *Trade in the New Independent States,* Studies of Economies in Transformation 13, edited by Constantine Michalopoulos and David G. Tarr, 1–20. Washington: World Bank.

Murphy, Kevin, Andrei Shleifer, and Robert Vishny. 1992. "The Transition to a Market Economy: Pitfalls of Partial Reform." *Quarterly Journal of Economics* 57 (August): 889–906.

Murrell, Peter. 1993. "What Is Shock Therapy? What Did It Do in Poland and Russia?" *Post-Soviet Affairs* 9 (April-June): 111–40.

Naughton, Barry. 1992. "Implications of the State Monopoly over Industry and Its Relaxation." *Modern China* 18 (January): 14–43.

Neven, Damien. Forthcoming. "Trade Liberalization with Eastern Nations: How Sensitive?" In *European Union Trade with Eastern Europe: Adjustment and Opportunities,* edited by Riccardo Faini and Richard Portes. London: Centre for Economic Policy Research.

Nuti, Domenico Mario, and Richard Portes. 1993. "Central Europe: The Way Forward." In *Economic Transformation in Central Europe: A Progress Report,* edited by Richard Portes, 1–20. London: Centre for Economic Policy Research.

Ofer, Gur. 1991. "Productivity, Competitiveness and the Socialist System." In *International Productivity and Competitiveness*, edited by Bert Hickman, 97–133. Oxford University Press.

———. 1992. "Stabilizing and Restructuring in the Former Soviet Economy: Big Bang or Gradual Sequencing?" In *Trials of Transition: Economic Reform in the Former Communist Bloc*, edited by Keren Michael and Gur Ofer, 150–75. Boulder, Colo.: Westview Press.

———. 1994. "Macroeconomic Stabilization and Structural Change: Orthodox, Heterodox, or Otherwise?" Paper presented at the IEA Congress, Moscow, 1992. In *Economics in a Changing World: Proceedings of the 10th World Congress of the International Economics Association, Moscow,* edited by Abel Aganbegyan, Oleg Bogomolov, and Michael Kaser, 87–111. Basingstoke: Macmillan.

Organization for Economic Cooperation and Development (OECD). 1990. *Foreign Trade by Commodity.* Paris.

———. 1993a. *OECD Economic Outlook* 53 (June). Paris.

———. 1993b. *OECD Economic Outlook* 54 (December). Paris.

———. 1994a. *Barriers to Trade with the Economies in Transition.* Paris.

———. 1994b. *Economic Survey, Czech and Slovak Republics.* Paris.

———. 1994c. *OECD Economic Outlook* 55 (June). Paris.

———. 1994d. *Short-Term Economic Indicators: Transition Economies,* 1/1994. Paris.

———. 1994e. *Short-Term Economic Indicators: Transition Economies,* 2/1994. Paris.

Ostry, Sylvia. 1993. "The Threat of Managed Trade to Transforming Economies." European Bank for Reconstruction and Development Working Paper 3. London.

Pinto, Brian, Marek Belka, and Stefan Krajewski. 1993. "Transforming State Enterprises in Poland: Evidence on Adjustment by Manufacturing Firms." *Brookings Papers on Economic Activity* 1: 213–61.

PlanEcon. 1992. *Review and Outlook: Analysis and Forecasts to 1996 of Economic Developments in the Former Soviet Republics.* Washington.

———. 1994a. *PlanEcon Report: Economic Recovery in the East* 9 (February 10).

———. 1994b. *PlanEcon Report: Russian Economic Monitor* 10 (April 28).

Porter, Michael, E. 1990. *The Competitive Advantage of Nations.* Macmillan.

Portes, Richard. 1991a. "Introduction." *European Economy.* Special edition 2: *The Path of Reform in Central and Eastern Europe,* 1–16.

———. 1991b. "The Transition to Convertibility for Eastern Europe and the USSR." In *Economics for the New Europe,* edited by Anthony B. Atkinson and Renato Brunetta, 89–98. London: Macmillan.

———. 1991c. "The European Community and Eastern Europe after 1992." In *Europe after 1992: Three Essays,* edited by Tommaso Padoa-Schioppa. Princeton Essays in International Finance 182. Princeton University Press.

———. 1992a. "The European Community's Response to Eastern Europe." In *The Economic Consequences of the East,* edited by Peter Bofinger. London: Centre for Economic Policy Research.

———. 1992b. "Is There a Better Way?" *International Economic Insights* 3 (May-June): 18–22.

———, ed. 1993a. *Economic Transformation in Central Europe: A Progress Report.* London: Centre for Economic Policy Research.

———. 1993b. "The Contraction of Eastern Europe's Economies" (comments on paper by Mario I. Blejer and Alan Gelb). In *Eastern Europe in Transition: From Recession to Growth*, edited by Mario I. Blejer and others, 8–11. Washington: World Bank.

———. 1994a. "Integrating the Central and East European Countries into the International Monetary System." Centre for Economic Policy Research Occasional Paper 14. London.

———. 1994b. "Transformation Traps." *Economic Journal* 104 (September): 1178–89.

———. 1994c. "Economic Liberalization and Reform: The Experience of Eastern Europe." Paper presented at IMF–World Bank conference, Madrid, 1994.

Radio Free Europe/Radio Liberty. 1994. *1993: The Year in Review.* January.

Rawski, Thomas. 1994. "Progress without Privatization: The Reform of China's State Industries." In *Changing Political Economy of Privatization in Post-Communist and Reforming Communist States,* edited by Vedat Milor, 150–75. Boulder, Colo.: Lynne Rienner Publishers.

Rodrik, Dani. 1992a. "Foreign Trade in Eastern Europe's Transition: Early Results." Centre for Economic Policy Research Discussion Paper 676 (June). London.

———. 1992b. "Making Sense of the Soviet Trade Shock in Eastern Europe." National Bureau of Economic Research Working Paper 4112. Cambridge, Mass.

Rosati, Dariusz K. 1992. "Problems of Post-CMEA Trade and Payments." In *Trade, Payments and Adjustment in Central and Eastern Europe,* edited by John Flemming and J. M. C. Rollo, 75–109. London: Royal Institute of International Affairs.

———. 1994. "Output Decline during Transition from Plan to Market: A Reconsideration." *Economics of Transition* 2: 419–41.

Sachs, Jeffrey. 1994a. "Prospects for Monetary Stabilization in Russia." In *Economic Transformation in Russia,* edited by Anders Aslund, 34–58. Harvard University Press.

———. 1994b. "Russia's Struggle with Economic Stabilization." Washington: World Bank.

Sachs, Jeffrey, and Wing Thye Woo. 1993. "Structural Factors in the Economic Reforms of China, Eastern Europe, and the Former Soviet Union." *Economic Policy* 18 (April): 101–45.

Sapir, André. 1995. "The Europe Agreements: Implications for Trade Laws and Institutions." In *Foundations of an Open Economy: Trade Laws and Institutions for Eastern Europe,* edited by L. Alan Winters. London: Centre for Economic Policy Research.

Tanzi, Vito, ed. 1993a. "Fiscal Policy and the Economic Restructuring of Economies in Transition." IMF Working Paper 22 (March). Washington.

———. 1993b. *Transition to Market: Studies in Fiscal Reform.* Washington: International Monetary Fund.

Tepluxin, P., and T. Normaka. 1994. " Trade between FSU States." In *Economic Survey of Russia,* 1993 IV, 181–205 (in Russian).

United Nations. 1994. Commodity Trade Database.

United Nations, Economic Commission for Europe. 1989. *Economic Bulletin for Europe* 45.

———. 1992. *Economic Bulletin for Europe* 44.

———. 1993. *Economic Bulletin for Europe* 41.

Universe. 1994. *Outlook: Financial Markets* 2. Moscow: Universe.

van Brabant, Joseph, M. 1993a. "The New East and Its Preferred Trade Regime— The Impact of Soviet Disintegration." In 103d Congress, 1st session, Joint Economic Committee, *Former Soviet Union in Transition* 1: 146–62 (February).

———. 1993b. "Ruble Convertibility, External and Internal Equilibrium." In 103d Congress, 1st session, Joint Economic Committee, *Former Soviet Union in Transition* 1: 422–38 (February).

Végh, Carlos A. 1991. "Stopping High Inflation: An Analytical Overview." IMF Working Paper 107 (November). Washington.

Wallich, Christine I. 1992. *Fiscal Decentralization: Intergovernmental Relations in Russia.* Washington: International Monetary Fund.

WEFA Group. 1992. *FCPE Outlook for Foreign Trade and Finance.* Philadephia: Wharton Econometric Forecasting.

Werner, Klaus. 1993. "Russia's Foreign Trade and the Economic Reforms." *Intereconomics* 28 (May-June): 144–52.

Whitlock, Erik. 1994. "The CIS Economies: Divergent and Troubled Paths." *Radio Free Europe, Radio Liberty Research Report* 3 (January): 13–17.

Williamson, John. 1991. *The Economic Opening of Eastern Europe.* Washington: Institute for International Economics.

Winters, L. Alan, ed. 1995. *Foundations of an Open Economy: Trade Laws and Institutions for Eastern Europe.* London: Centre for Economic Policy Research.

Woo, Wing Thye. 1993. "The Art of Reforming Centrally-Planned Economies: Comparing China, Poland and Russia." Paper presented at the Asia Foundation conference, Transition of Centrally Planned Economies in Pacific Asia, San Francisco.

Woo, Wing Thye, and others. 1993. "How Successful Has Chinese Enterprise Reform Been?" Paper presented at the Asia Foundation conference, Transition of Centrally Planned Economies in Pacific Asia, San Francisco.

World Bank. 1992. *China: Reform and the Role of the Plan in the 1990s.* Washington.

———. 1993a. *Historically Planned Economies: A Guide to the Data.* Washington.

———. 1993b. *Russia Joining the World Economy.* Washington.

———. 1993c. *Statistical Handbook, 1993: States of the Former USSR.* Studies of Economies in Transformation 8. Washington.

———. 1993d. *World Debt Tables 1993–94: External Debt of Developing Countries,* vol. 2. Washington.

———. 1993e. *World Development Report 1993.* Oxford University Press.

———. 1994a. *China: Foreign Trade Reform.* Washington.

———. 1994b. *World Tables 1993.* Johns Hopkins University Press.

Index